War
Crimes

First published in 2014

A catalogue record for this book is available from the British Library

ISBN: 978-0-85733-669-9

Published by Haynes Publishing, Sparkford, Yeovil,
Somerset BA22 7JJ, UK
Tel: 01963 442030 Fax: 01963 440001
Int. tel: +44 1963 442030 Int. fax: +44 1963 440001
E-mail: sales@haynes.co.uk
Website: www.haynes.co.uk

Haynes North America Inc., 861 Lawrence Drive, Newbury Park, California 91320, USA

Images © Mirrorpix

Creative Director: Kevin Gardner
Designed for Haynes by BrainWave

Printed and bound in the US

War
Crimes

From The Case Files of

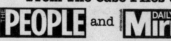

Claire Welch

Contents

Introduction

At the beginning of September 2013, top of the international agenda was to stop any further deadly chemical attacks on the people of Syria. Bringing the war criminals to justice was not far behind. A United Nations commission was already in place to investigate abuses committed by all sides, and it probed 14 illegal chemical attacks including one that killed more than 1,400 people. Maher al-Assad, the brother of Syria's President, Bashar al-Assad, was thought to be behind the atrocities. Reports claimed that the ruthless Republican Guard ordered a junior captain to fire chemical shells under threat of being shot in the head. Other suspected perpetrators included Assad's brother-in-law, General Assef Shawkat, head of Syrian military intelligence, and cousin, Rami Makhlouf.

History is littered with brutal war crimes and the criminals behind them, and many have been brought to justice. Iraqi tyrant Saddam Hussein was hanged, while Serbian Slobodan Milošević died in his prison cell of a heart attack following his arrest and having charges brought against him for war crimes. Libya suffered under Colonel Gaddafi, while Bosnia saw war crimes perpetrated by Ratko Mladić. Germany, however, has had to come to terms with some of the worst atrocities and crimes committed by humankind, and there is now speculation that up to 30 concentration camp guards could finally face justice for the deaths of helpless men, women and children who were murdered in the gas chambers, or shot as they desperately tried to escape across barbed wire. Led by German lawyers, there are moves being made to see that surviving Nazis should pay for their horrific crimes before they die. More than 1.1 million people were killed between 1941 and 1945 at the Auschwitz-Birkenau camp in southern Poland, while a total of 11 million people were slaughtered in unimaginable circumstances during the Holocaust as a whole. Lower-ranking Nazis, guards, overseers and those that "arrested" Jews and other victimized groups were allowed to literally get away with murder. However, despite the outcry over the Holocaust and the bombing of Hiroshima, the committing of war crimes has continued into the 21st century.

The 20th century is depressingly war-stained, but nations have agreed that international courts should be established to deter and punish the worst crimes against humanity. These courts enforce new laws against violations of human rights yet still fail to deter these atrocities from happening. Governments and victims seek justice, and revenge is not uncommon. However, whether war crimes are the result of bad leadership, manipulation or the pursuit of political power, or whether they are rooted in religious, ethnic or historical animosities is still undecided.

The Khmer Rouge terrorized the Cambodian people between 1975 and 1979. While under their rule, more than a million people died of starvation, disease, torture and execution. Despite the fact that the Khmer Rouge was overthrown more than 30 years ago, their legacy meant that Cambodians suffered economically, psychologically and politically for many years afterwards. In the 1990s there was mass genocide in Rwanda, while in South Africa apartheid enforced racial segregation and economic and social control that saw millions of people being forced to relocate. Just two months after the international agenda highlighted the plight of the Serbian people, the British Prime Minister, David Cameron, slammed what was going on in Sri Lanka on 14th November 2013. Mr Cameron was embroiled in a furious diplomatic row with Sri Lanka as he jetted in to the country for the mid-November Commonwealth summit. The Prime Minister lashed out at "appalling and chilling" war-crime atrocities carried out by government forces in the country. He made the remarks just hours before touching down in Colombo, and was set to further inflame tensions when he was expected to become the first world leader to visit Sri Lanka's war-torn north. Cameron was due to visit a refugee camp in Jaffna, home to Sri Lanka's persecuted Tamil minority. His explosive intervention in the country's turmoil came after Sri Lanka's hard-man President Mahinda Rajapaksa hit out at the Prime Minister's bid to use the Commonwealth heads of government meeting to "shine a spotlight" on Sri Lanka's war record. The Sri Lanka leader said he had "nothing to hide", adding: "I will be meeting him and we will see what. I will also have to ask some questions. If anyone wants to complain about a human rights violation in Sri Lanka – whether it be torture, whether it be rape – we have a system." Mr Cameron responded to Mr Rajapaksa's remarks after touching down in Calcutta from Delhi on 14th November 2013. The Prime Minister confirmed he was preparing for "a frank exchange of views" with Mr Rajapaksa. He said: "There are some important points to put to the Sri Lankans. There is the problem of human rights as we speak today – the people who have disappeared, the lack of free rights for journalists and a free press. But I think perhaps most important of all is the need for proper investigations to look into what happened at the end of this very long, appalling civil war that took place and these appalling scenes that we've seen on our television screens of people being killed. The images are completely chilling. It's an appalling set of allegations and of course these allegations have been backed up by the work of the UN Special Rapporteur who has had them verified. These are chilling images of appalling acts and they need to be properly investigated. There are legitimate accusations of war crimes that need to be properly investigated." Mr Cameron said the government had not "effectively answered" what went on. He said: "There are some very serious questions that need to be answered." Mr Cameron's focus on Sri Lanka's human rights abuses was likely to overshadow the start of the summit. Government forces – representing the island's dominant Sinhalese majority – allegedly slaughtered up to 40,000 ethnic Tamil civilians in the closing stages of the almost four-decade-long conflict in the island's north.

Fleet Street Fox (with the tag line "Often sarcastic. Occasionally right") wrote a poignant piece in the *Daily Mirror* on

11th November 2013. It read: "We're still at war and there are still people who want us to hate. Poppies only grow if you disturb their seeds. That's why, when trenches were dug all across northern France in the First World War, they blossomed into a sea of red. They're delicate things, poppies, with silky petals that are easily torn. Even more easily than that war sent 9 million men and boys – many of them volunteers – to their deaths in the mud. It was a long time ago, that slaughter, and poppies don't mean so much to 21st-century people for whom war consists of video game-style drone strikes on the evening news. Some people care enough to wear a poppy for remembrance, and today more than 300 of them turned out to the funeral of Harold Percival.

"In the Second World War Harold worked at RAF Bomber Command, that body of people who delivered the 'bouncing bomb' that destroyed the dams providing power to the enemy's armaments factories. Civilians were killed, innocents suffered, but the Dambusters helped to turn the tide of a war being fought for the best of reasons – to protect freedom. Harold had no friends, never married, had no children and, at 99, no close family living to mourn him. After a campaign, many people turned out in the rain on Armistice Day to say thank you to Harold, and see him on his way. His coffin was draped in the Union flag, and they played the Dambusters theme tune. *People do remember, and people do care*. But it's considered an old man's game, that sort of war, and despite the selfless act of those at Harold's funeral there are fewer of us wearing poppies this year. Last year the Poppy

Appeal, which raises money to help veterans, missed its target by £3m. The fad for jeweled poppies which don't fall off your coat every five minutes means as little as 10 per cent of the cost goes to charity. And for two or three weeks a year, everywhere you turn there's a politician or celebrity shoving a poppy in your face. Newsreaders, *X Factor* judges, daytime TV hosts. Whether they wear it with sincerity or not, the fact they MUST be worn makes them seem insincere. We all know a poppy gets crumpled after a day or two – yet those on-screen are pristine, unloved, worn for the look of the thing rather than the point of it. I was in a TV studio the other day and the floor manager bustled over with a tray of poppies to pin one on automatically. He didn't even ask for a donation. *I wear my poppy with pride, but I will not wear one because someone tells me to or because the Prime Minister does.*

"It's 99 years since the First World War began, and those poppy seeds were first disturbed in Flanders fields – Harold Percival's entire lifetime. Now that he and others like him are gone, our collective memory about why we do this is fading. It's not just for old men. It's not just to turn out at funerals for those who fought for our freedom a long time ago. My great-uncle was killed in the Second World War, and my grandfather was never the same when he came home. When I was growing up, I wore a poppy for them. Because it had been horrible and I was glad it wasn't me. A few years ago a friend of mine was blown up in Afghanistan, and another lost both legs. They were targeted by the Taliban because they were journalists, and now I wear my poppy for them too. Those two big wars we were taught about as children were not the end. Harold's help to smash the dams stopped Hitler, but there are plenty more just like him, propagating hate. There are the fascists of fundamentalism, and on a smaller scale there are those who say we should not trust people who are different. Migrants, Muslims, Romanians, Poles, those who cannot work, the disabled, the sick and the poor. All our problems get blamed on them. It's not the same as being a Nazi, but it's not a long way off. And don't think for a moment that the oxymoronically-named War on Terror isn't a Third World War. It's affecting most of the countries on the planet at the moment, and that's the only qualification it needs. Just because we are not up to our waists in mud and being shot at doesn't mean it doesn't affect us in ways that are more meaningful than having to take your belt off at airport security. The free world is cutting back on its human rights laws. It's launching drone strikes that kill civilians, and radicalise the survivors. Our enemies look just like people who are our friends, and the Reich they want to build is even worse than the last one. They won't win – hate never does, in the long run – but for some reason we are not disturbed enough by all the dangers surrounding us to grow into a people who think we ought to be united. Muslims died for Britain in the first and second world wars, you know. Poles packed out the RAF, immigrants and those who could not or did not work joined up and did their bit. They knew, and we do not remember, that freedom is as delicate as a poppy's petals, and easily torn. It's destroyed by hate, mistrust, insincerity, by corrupt politicians and by bad journalists. The poppy should be worn just one day a year – one powerful, important day, when we stand together against death and hate and mud and horror. And we should spend the other 364 trying, very hard, not to go back there. Lest we forget – it will come around again."

Writing towards the end of August 2013, just three days after the suspected chemical attack on Syria, broadcaster and journalist Mark Austen wrote under the heading "Sickening horror in Syria while the world keeps its eyes wide shut" that: "On the most basic level, it is sickening that, if proved to be the work of the Assad regime, a despot could do this to his own people. It doesn't take much. Just a few clicks of a mouse. And there it is. The barbarous depravity of the Syrian civil war, right there on your laptop. Once seen, they are images that are hard to erase from the mind. Scores of victims, many of them children, convulsing, foaming at the mouth and shaking uncontrollably. And others, lifeless and staring blankly as medics try frantically to save them using hand-pump respirators.

"Within 24 hours of the alleged chemical weapons attack taking place in the eastern suburbs of the Syrian capital Damascus, I counted no fewer than 130 different videos of the horror uploaded on to YouTube. In a conflict that has been characterized by harrowing amateur videos of atrocities, these are surely the most gut-wrenchingly ghastly yet seen. And the *Daily*

Mirror front page earlier this week captured the horror and was necessarily shocking. Syria is now sickening on so many levels.

"It is also sickening that, such are the depths of depravity reached in Syria, it's even being suggested that rebel fighters could have staged the attack themselves to try to provoke intervention by the West. What sort of warped propaganda war is that? It is sickening, of course, that it has been allowed to get this far. An Arab Spring, pro-democracy uprising by unarmed protesters has become a blood-drenched civil war that has been hijacked by extremist jihadist groups linked to al-Qaeda. Real pressure early on would have made life far more difficult for President Assad. Instead, what happened? His backers, Russia and China, blocked resolution after resolution against the regime. Moscow – a major arms supplier to Syria – used its veto at the UN to stymie calls for sanctions, an arms embargo and moves to refer Assad and his henchmen to the International Criminal Court.

"It is sickening that the UN has proved itself an utterly inadequate, feeble body that has totally failed in its duty. The UN Security Council charter demands 'prompt and effective action' to protect vulnerable people. In the case of Syria, it has done neither. The pathetic initial response to the chemical atrocity sums up the weakness of the UN. It expressed 'strong concern' and called for 'greater clarity'. How President Assad must be quaking in his blood-soaked boots. And it is not only Syria."

He continues: "I had the misfortune to be in Rwanda in 1994 when the UN stood by and watched as an estimated

750,000 people were massacred in three genocidal months. And I was in Bosnia nine years later when 8,000 Muslim men were slaughtered in what was supposed to be the safety of a UN haven. So the UN has form and what it really needs is reform. But what is most sickening of all is the unerring feeling that nothing can be done to stop the slaughter taking place in Syria now. Any suggestion of intervention by bombing or invasion could ignite an even wider conflict. And it could also hand victory to just the sort of extremists the West is committed to fighting. So click away. Look at the horror of Syria. It's easy. Far harder, though, to see a way out of it."

Mark Austen also wrote about the "true picture" of war-torn countries and the "cost" war caused for not just those living in it, but for those working on the front lines to make sure that the rest of the world knows just how atrocities are being metered out. Austen states: "Showing the true picture cost my mate Mick Deane his life." He writes in the same article in 2013: "There's an old saying among TV correspondents that you're only as good as your cameraman. TV news is driven by pictures and great pictures make for powerful television. Mick Deane was taking pictures of the army assault on protesters in Cairo when his life was cruelly cut short by a sniper's bullet. Mick stood out. He was a big, blonde, loveable bear of a man. No sniper in his right mind could have mistaken him for a participant. No, he would have known what Mick was doing. So I can only conclude that he was deliberately targeted. And that would make Mick Deane's death not only a tragic waste, but also a crime. I fear for our trade."

Where once the independence and neutrality of the media was recognized and respected, now it's clear that journalists are increasingly being targeted by those who fear the truth emerging. Blaming the messenger is not enough these days. Silencing the messenger is now the name of the game. It is a horrific truth that 70 per cent of the journalists killed in the last two decades have been killed intentionally. And here is another scandalous statistic. In 80 per cent of those cases the killers have never been brought to justice.

Austen continues: "Mick Deane always believed in 'being there', bearing witness, and hoping his pictures might make a difference. But increasingly there is a high price to pay. I can't believe he's gone. We spent several years in the nineties travelling the world together. On one assignment we went undercover in North Korea, posing as teachers. Mick had filled in the forms, saying he was a geography teacher and, for me, he put down maths, knowing that it was my worst subject at school. How he laughed when, during a visit to a school in Pyongyang, I was invited to take a maths lesson. Mick was so much more than a cameraman. He was my guiding hand and a wise and shrewd companion. At 61, he was looking forward to retirement with his wife, Daniella. He deserved it and he longed for it. Until that sniper had him in his sights."

However, there are those that "fight" for the cause of those who carry out war crimes and even represent them in the judicial process. The lawyer known as the "Devil's Advocate" for defending some of the world's most notorious killers died at the age of 88. French barrister Jacques Verges represented infamous clients including Nazi war criminal Klaus Barbie and terrorist Carlos the Jackal. Verges, who died of a heart attack in Paris on 15th August 2013, also advised former Yugoslav leader Slobodan Milošević, and offered his legal services to ex-Iraqi dictator Saddam Hussein. This charismatic man was born in Thailand in 1925 to a French father and Vietnamese mother. He grew up on the French-ruled Indian Ocean island of Réunion. He joined the French Resistance when he was 17, and was marching to liberate Paris from the Nazis in 1944 when Barbie, the evil Gestapo chief known as the "Butcher of Lyon", fled the country. Verges baffled compatriots by representing Barbie in 1987 when he was convicted of crimes against humanity.

Verges said in 2002: "If he had been at the end of the barrel of my gun [in 1944] I would have shot him." He added: "Now I am simply doing my job as a lawyer." In 2008 he said: "I told Barbie… 'You're not a monster'. When you treat the accused as a monster, you give up trying to understand what happened. And if you don't try to understand what happened, you deprive yourself of any reflection on how to stop that thing happening elsewhere."

In his student days Verges befriended Pol Pot, who became the Khmer Rouge leader and was responsible for the Cambodian genocide in which 2 million died. Verges went on to defend ex-Khmer Rouge head of state Khieu Samphan and once said he would even have acted as defence lawyer for Adolf Hitler.

In March 2013 Scotland Yard investigated 29 alleged war criminals living in Britain – including five suspected Nazis who were thought to have been in hiding since the Second World War. A memo seen by the *Daily Mirror* revealed how the Home Office had made a total of 47 referrals to counter-terrorism unit SO15, of which 29 suspects were interrogated. However, it left a huge discrepancy between the number of people the Home Office suspects of war crimes and those investigated by police. In 2012, immigration officials at the UK Border Agency recommended action against 207 war crime suspects. Yet only one in four of the fugitives was referred to Scotland Yard. There was no dedicated war crimes unit, and the caseload had been taken up by just eight senior detectives inside SO15. One of the men under SO15 investigation was Mohamed Salim, who admitted to being involved in genocide in his native Sudan. The *Daily Mirror* exposed how he was living on benefits in Birmingham. Salim, 27, gave an anonymous interview to the BBC's *Newsnight* team after arriving in Britain in 2006. He said at the time: "Whenever we go into a village and find resistance, we kill everyone. Most were civilians. Most were women. Innocent people running out and being killed – including children."

SO15 was funded by the Office for Security and Counter-Terrorism, but there was no ring-fenced budget to tackle the investigation of war criminals living in Britain. Labour MP Michael McCann, chairman of the All-Party Parliamentary Group for the

Prevention of Genocide and Crimes against Humanity said: "Put simply, the Border Agency and SO15 figures are strangers to each other. I've asked the Home Secretary for an independent inquiry into these figures. But on top of that we must look once again at setting up a bespoke war crimes police unit to ensure war criminals cannot have safe haven here. The British public will accept nothing less." International criminals living in Britain in 2013 included mass murderers, torturers and rapists, some of whom could not be deported because they faced torture in their home countries. The fugitives, many of them asylum seekers, were mainly from Afghanistan, Iraq, Rwanda, Sierra Leone, Sri Lanka and Zimbabwe. However, SO15 had five open cases relating to war crimes from the Second World War as well. The five suspected Nazis were thought to have fled to Britain in 1945. In 2011, pensioner Alexander Huryn from Farnham, Hampshire, was quizzed by Scotland Yard after it emerged that he had been a Nazi guard at a Polish labour camp. It was thought that no further action should be taken against him. Huryn, 90, who was thought to be still living in a retirement home, said at the time: "I do feel bad about what we had to do – I didn't like it, but I did nothing wrong at all."

SO15 had so far only charged one person – Colonel Kumar Lama, 46, a Nepalese army officer facing trial for torture during his country's civil war in 2005. Police said the charges related to two alleged incidents at Gorusinghe army barracks in Nepal. The Aegis Trust, an anti-war crimes and genocide charity, called for the government to take action against all suspects trying to hide in the UK. Dr James Smith said: "The Home Office shouldn't accept that there's a case against someone for war crimes and then do nothing about it." Meanwhile, police were probing Salim's involvement in the killings of "countless" civilians in Sudan. He was found living in a rent-free semi-detached house while getting £160 a month from the taxpayer. SO15 were understood to be "aware" of his past as a Janjaweed fighter – who had taken part in attacks on villages in Darfur in Western Sudan, during which women and children were burned alive.

This book takes a detailed and disturbing look at some of the worst atrocities ever committed by humankind and questions whether war crimes might one day become catastrophic events that can be confined firmly to the past.

The First World War

1914–1918

The "Huns" massacred 80 children, according to newspaper reports on 15th September 1914. The *Central News* in Paris reported on the previous day that a German giving evidence in Basel, Switzerland, gave the following account of the destruction of the village of Burzweiler, known as Bourtzwiller to the French, by German forces: "A detachment of Germans entered Burzweiler to pass the night, the inhabitants giving up their beds. Later there arrived more soldiers, who camped near the village. An army horse had been wounded, and the captain, to shorten the beast's suffering, caused it to be killed. Hearing the shot, a sentry gave the alarm, and thinking that the enemy was at the gates, the soldiers who had been asleep began firing from the windows. The Germans quartered outside entered Burzweiler and opened fire on their own comrades, afterwards setting fire to the village and causing the deaths of 80 innocent children in the flames." *Central News* said: "In addition, numerous inhabitants were shot."

The following year, on 6th February, it was cited in newspapers that: "The atrocious cruelty of the German army in Belgium receives terrible illustrations in the report, issued yesterday, of the Commission of Inquiry on the violation of the Rules of International Law and of the Laws and Customs of War." At

Surice, with the village burning around them, a group of around 50 or 60 people, both men and women, were driven together. The 18 men who had been herded were then separated from the women and told that they were to be shot. Fathers and sons stood side by side, awaiting their fate, while opposite, their wives and daughters looked on in terror. Many were wailing. Many were praying. Many were doing both. A volley of machine gun fire took the men down. They fell together watched by their loved ones in a truly barbaric massacre.

In 1917, on 5th March, German troops massacred 60 Russian prisoners of war. A Reuter's telegram from Petrograd to Paris stated that M Krivtsoff, a member of the Senate and President of the Extraordinary Commission of Inquiry on German Atrocities, had published a report, which he guaranteed was genuine. The report stated that on 9th October 1916, 60 Russian non-commissioned officers and 250 enlisted men were brought as prisoners of war to Mannheim. Five days later a German officer told them they were to be employed at a military works in northern France, and asked the non-commissioned officers if they consented to go. When the German officer received numerous protests, he called a detachment of German soldiers and ordered them to beat the Russian non-commissioned officers with the butt ends of their rifles. It took the German troops one and a half hours to beat the 60 Russians to death in this way. When the massacre was complete, the German officer mounted the heap of corpses and walked about on top of the bodies for quite some time.

There were appalling tales of cruelty in South-West Africa between 1904 and 1907, which only came to light in September 1918. According to newspaper reports, the Germans were responsible for "revolting practices" in the region. A report by Mr E H M Gorges, the administrator of the then colony, told how "an unbroken record of German bad faith", culminated in the great Herero and Hottentot rebellions of 1904 and 1907. Women were habitually maltreated by German troops, who also forced them into sex slavery. In the end the local people were deliberately goaded into rebellions, which were then suppressed with characteristic cruelty that resulted in the executions of the tribes involved. The full effect of the principle of "colonization by extermination", was gathered from figures before and after the rebellions. It was one of the most tragic and grim incidents in the history of South-West Africa. As a result, Leutwein, who was regarded as "too lenient," was superseded by General von Trotha, who played a notorious part in the Chinese Boxer Rebellion and was responsible for suppressing the Arab rebellion in German East Africa, which included the wholesale massacre of men, women and children. Trotha, on completing his plans, issued an "extermination order", in which no Herero was to receive mercy. He said: "Kill every one of them, and take no prisoners." The orders were faithfully carried out as one eyewitness stated: "On one occasion, I saw about 25 prisoners placed in a small enclosure of thorn bushes. They were confined in a very small space, and the soldiers cut dry branches and piled dry logs all round them – men, women and children and little girls were there. Having piled up the branches, lamp oil was sprinkled on the heap and it was set on fire. The prisoners were burnt to a cinder. I saw this personally." In another incident, German troops sent out messages to the native Hereros that the war was over and that they were to come to a farm called Otjihaenena, where they could make peace. As a result, seven Herero leaders visited the German camp to discuss peace terms. Here they were led to a spot, tied up with ropes and shot. Trotha's native ex-groom described the incident where the seven peace envoys were shot, and also told how he had once been ordered to kill a young Herero woman who had been captured. He refused in disgust, but a soldier laughed and said: "If you won't do it, I will show you what a German soldier can do." He took the woman aside and drove a bayonet through her body. The ex-groom said: "He then withdrew the bayonet and brought it all dropping with blood and poked it under my nose in a jeering way, saying: 'You see, I have done it.'" At the same time, newspapers stated that a number of photographs of the injuries inflected on certain women were also published in the report.

On 17th March 1919, the catalogue of crimes compiled by the Allied War Guilt Commission, according to one of the sub-committees, comprised a list of no fewer than 30 varieties of crime, which newspapers said would "for centuries to come blacken the names of Germany and her associates". The list included the following:

Massacre of civilians

Putting hostages to death

Torture of civilians

Starvation

Rape

Abduction of girls and women for purposes of enforced
prostitution

Deportation

Internment of civilians under brutal conditions

Putting civilians to forced labour in connection with military
operations of the enemy

Usurpation of sovereignty during military occupation

Compulsory enlistment of soldiers among inhabitants of
occupied territory

Pillage

Confiscation of property

Exaction of illegitimate requisitions

Debasement of currency and issue of spurious currency

Imposition of collective penalties

Wanton devastation

Bombardment of undefended places

Wanton destruction of religious, charitable, educational and
historical buildings and monuments

Destruction of merchant ships and passenger vessels
without warning

Destruction of fishing boats and of relief ships

Bombardment of hospitals

Destruction of hospital ships

Breach of other rules relating to the Red Cross

Use of gases

Use of explosive and expanding bullets

Directions to give no quarter

Ill-treatment of prisoners of war

Misuse of flags of truce

Poisoning of wells

At the beginning of June 1921, the third of a series of trials of Germans charged with war crimes was due to start. The accused, Robert Neumann, was a guard in a "working camp" attached to the chemical factory at Pommersdorf, near Stettin. Sergeant Major Trink'e, believed to be the main culprit in the case, was supposed to have fled to Poland. The fourth and last of the trials, in which British subjects were concerned, was fixed for a few days later. Karl Neumann, commander of the German submarine *U-67*, was charged with torpedoing and sinking the hospital ship *Dover Castle* off the north coast of Africa on 26th May 1917. The point of the trial was to establish whether the accused was justified by the orders of his superior officers, which practically authorized the sinking of hospital ships on the grounds that they were also carrying munitions.

After the German invasion of Belgium in August 1914, troops carried out mass atrocities against the civilian population –

known as the Rape of Belgium – in order to "flush out" Belgian guerrilla fighters in the first two months of the First World War. The occupation, which came without warning, was in German defiance of the 1907 Hague Convention on Land Warfare. No prosecutions were ever made, but soldiers willingly carried out the destruction of civilian property, looted and routinely carried out cold-blooded executions of men, women and children.

In 1915, the Ottoman Empire ordered the wholesale extermination of a minority of Armenians living within Anatolia. The Young Turk regime carried out the massacres of Armenians using military force, or deported them to Syria before they were massacred. More than 1.5 million Armenians were executed through genocide. The massacre of Armenians was carried out during two phases, both during the First World War and afterwards in the year following the end of conflict. Men were forced into labour, where many died from the extreme working conditions, while women and children were sent on death marches to Syria. The Ottoman government also carried out war crimes against other minority groups, which resulted in what became known as the Armenian Genocide. Today, it is acknowledged as one of the first modern-day genocides.

It was carried out at the same time as the first attack in the Baralong Incidents, where a German submarine, *U-27*, was sunk by the British Q-ship HMS *Baralong*. It was 19th August 1915, and Lieutenant Godfrey Herbert ordered his crew to kill the German survivors, including those that managed to board the British freighter, *Nicosian*. The German submarine had been preparing to sink the *Nicosian* when it was attacked, and eyewitnesses on board the British vessel reported the massacre of German survivors. HMS *Baralong* was at the heart of a second incident in September 1915 when it destroyed another German submarine, *U-41*, which was in the process of sinking another ship. Lieutenant Herbert ordered his crew to massacre the remaining survivors who had managed to board a lifeboat. These war crimes also brought no prosecutions.

In August 1916 newspapers were full of the atrocities being carried out against the Armenians. Reports mentioned the massacre of at least 500,000, while it was estimated that more than 1 million people had been deported. The appalling facts were brought to light in the UK by the Reverend Harold Buxton, the honorary secretary of the Armenian Refugees' (Lord Mayor's) Fund. He arrived in Britain after three months of relief work in the devastated vilayets. "The German government did nothing to stop the massacres", said Buxton in an interview. "During the whole business German influence was supreme at Constantinople, and German Consuls were at their posts in all the chief centres through Asia Minor", he went on. "Besides, the people were swept away with a methodical thoroughness, which one does not expect from the Turk, who, when left to himself, acts rather with sudden spasms of fury." He continued: "I have evidence from an American missionary that certain of the German Consuls did their best on behalf of the Armenian people. For instance, the German

Consul at Erzerum wired to his Ambassador at Constantinople vigorously protesting at the order for deportation. He received a reply in these words: 'We cannot interfere in the internal affairs of Turkey.'

"Groups of survivors are discovered here and there, but I don't think there has been any exaggeration as to the losses as published in England. The Armenian race numbered over 4,000,000. Of the 2,000,000 Turkish Armenians, perhaps 1,000,000 have been deported and 500,000 massacred. Only 200,000 escaped into the mountains and so across to Russian soil. These are the people we are helping to relieve. There are some hundreds of thousands in concentration camps between Aleppo and Mogul and in the neighbouring regions of Mesopotamia, where Turkey continues to be supreme over their fate." The interview continues with Reverend Buxton stating that it was believed many Armenians were employed as forced labour on the Baghdad Railway. These people, he believed, were in great danger and had no access to relief workers. He said: "According to reports which come through, it is being ravaged by sickness, famine, privations of every kind, outrages and murder, all of which means a high mortality among the victims." He continued: "Although the Bishops and clergy persuaded the people to give up their arms, and so exercised a restraining influence, many of those clergy have been barbarously murdered with the rest." Of those murdered, names included the Bishops Maloyan of Mardin, Israelian of Kharput and the Bishop of Erzerum, but there were many others. The population of Zeitun had maintained its independence, but agreed to disarm. Having done so, the entire population was promptly deported, while the women and girls who were totally defenceless were subjected to cruelty and killed outright when they refused the requests of their captors. Reverend Buxton called for immediate help for the survivors, especially as the winter of 1916 approached, and confirmed that around £80,000 had been collected for the relief fund, of which £57,000 was raised by the Lord Mayor's Fund. Arthur Balfour, writing to the American Committee for Armenian Relief, said: "The sufferings of the Armenians in the Ottoman Empire are known, but it is doubtful if their true horror is realized." He continued: "Those who were massacred died under abominable tortures, but they escaped the longer agonies of the deported. Men, women and children, without food or other provision for the journey, were driven from their homes and made to march as long as their strength lasted, or until those who drove them drowned or massacred them in batches. This bare recital of facts reveals the hideous cruelty of which they have been the victims: no words are needed to colour or to heighten the description."

Three years later, on 3rd January 1919, the "shocking atrocities" were being attributed to General Liman von Sanders of the German army. The *Petit Parisian* reported that the inquiry into the massacres held in Constantinople cited that von Sanders, along with Enver Pasha, Talaat Pasha and Djemal Pasha, were chiefly responsible for the crimes. A total of 50 per cent of the

Armenian population had been slaughtered, with the massacre having been "scientifically organized" by Germany. It was reported that among "other terrible incidents" was "that of the outraging and mutilating of 2,000 women by Kurds", who proceeded to smear their victims with petrol and set them on fire with a view to securing the jewels, which they were believed to have swallowed. In one area alone, more than 7,000 children were systematically executed, and numbers of children were buried alive. Some 14 months later, Reuters quoted stories of massacres of Armenians at Marash from the diary of a man named Mr Crathern, one of the American relief workers, who had been stranded when the mission compound in which he worked was placed under siege for 22 days. As Armenians fled through the streets they were shot down. "Some of them dropped wounded at our feet," said Mr Crathern, "others staggered into the compound with wild eyes and distorted faces, telling of the awful massacres which were just beginning". Another entry in the diary stated: "News came today that scores of women and children – a hundred in one house – had been butchered with knives and hatchets. After the men had been taken outside and shot, the women surrendered under promises of protection, but were betrayed." On 27th January 1920, Crathern wrote: "There is a young woman in our house who relates how she passed five nights praying in a cellar with a hundred others. The Turks asked them to surrender, promising their lives would be spared. They agreed, and the woman's husband went first and was immediately shot by their own Turkish neighbour. All the 80 girls in the rescue home were killed today, the Turks afterwards firing the building. We had to watch without being able to raise a hand to help."

It was a desperate situation before French relief troops arrived. The French commander announced his intention to evacuate the city, which caused "frantic and desperate" Armenians to determinedly leave the city at the same time as the French so as to avoid another major massacre. The mass of people moved in a column for a 75-mile trek in bitter weather conditions, and many of the weak dropped by the wayside to freeze or starve to death. It was estimated that more than 1,000 refugees perished before reaching the safety of İslahiye. Crathern estimated that around 20,000 Armenians perished in Marash. By 11th March 1920, it was thought that around three quarters of the Armenians had been killed. The race was on to save the tens of thousands of men, women and children that remained in "deadly danger". That same day, a peace conference was held in Britain and the British public was urged to form committees, hold meetings and write to their MPs demanding that the conference would spare the Armenians and all other minority groups from further bloodshed. Crathern also wrote: "Surely no one in the outside world can realize the seriousness of our situation? Is this to go on? Will you pass by on the other side while a nation is being cruelly and barbarously stamped out of existence?" It was reported that the Turkish policy towards the Armenians had always been "a policy of slaughter". The newspapers quoted Abdul Hamid, who said:

"The way to get rid of the Armenian question is to get rid of the Armenians." The *Daily Mirror* wrote: "The history of Turkish rule over Christians in Europe has ever been a history of continuous oppression and almost continuous outrage and massacre. The Powers protested from time to time, but they protested ineffectually. Diplomatic and financial intrigue in Europe proved stronger than the appeals of humanity and justice. Are they to prove stronger today?"

The massacres were described as the most hideous crime in history. Viscount Bryce, a writer noted for his sound judgment, said that: "three-fourths or four-fifths of the whole nation has been wiped out, and there is no case in history… in which any crime so hideous and upon so large a scale has been recorded." He wrote: "The Turks, as rulers, have proved themselves to be savages. They are, moreover, irreclaimable savages. Their governing class… is cruel, perfidious, incapable of honest or efficient government, dead to all feelings of justice or humanity." It was felt that the only way to stop the butchery was to stop Turkish rule over "subject peoples". The newspapers stated: "Can you in honour leave the Armenian who fought for you at the mercy of the Turk who fought against you – the Turk, whose alliance with Germany prolonged the war at the cost of thousands of British lives?" An article in the *Daily Mirror* continued: "Religious bigotry does not enter into this matter. No one wishes to destroy the Turk, or even to do any injustice to him. It is fully recognized that the Turks themselves have a perfect right to their own form of government, so long as their exercise of it does not involve the murder of innocent human beings. No sort of persecution of the Turks is intended. What is intended is that the Turk shall be prevented from persecuting." One eyewitness described the plight of the Armenians by saying: "The weazened skins of these refugees cling in fear to their rattling bones. Just human remnants... not protected from the elements by even the dignity of rags. They are pencil sketches of humanity." Dr Mabel Elliott, a missionary besieged in Marash said: "No language that I could use could exaggerate the horror of the scenes that I witnessed. The Turks slaughtered the Armenians wherever they found them... the wounded crawled into the hospital from the street covered with blood – one poor old woman who was shot through the lung, thigh and ankle managed to get to us though the flesh was taken off her knees down to the bone through crawling through the streets – the wife of the Armenian Protestant Pastor came in with three gunshot wounds and four terrible stabs – her two children had been knifed before her eyes; she had another baby, poor woman, as soon as she got into the hospital, and died within 48 hours. Her case was only one of hundreds. Whole families were slaughtered, babies killed in cold blood." Elliott also described the hell of the trek to İslahiye and said: "There was a terrible blizzard – we struggled on – people were literally dropping dead on all sides – every few yards one passed a shapeless bundle in the snow, and one was glad if it did not move." The British public was urged to donate as much as they could to the Lord Mayor's Fund.

The First World War was the first major international conflict following the Hague Convention of 1907, which heralded some focus on war crimes and crimes against humanity, including torture and genocide.

The Second World War

1939–1945

"Two thousand Rumanian Iron Guard members have paid with their lives for the life of Premier Călinescu, who was assassinated by a member of the Nazi-inspired organization which he had ruthlessly suppressed", said the *Daily Mirror* on 23rd September 1939. Swift, merciless Balkan justice had been meted out in a series of "mass execution parties" in Bucharest, the capital, and all over the country, while the formality of trial was ignored. Thousands of Iron Guard "terrorists" and suspects were thrown into concentration camps. Eight members of the Iron Guard were arrested immediately after the Prime Minister's assassination. At 11.00 pm, on a Thursday night, they were transported by police to the spot where they had murdered Călinescu and, with the same guns they had used to kill the premier, they themselves were shot by a firing squad. It was announced that 44 members of the Iron Guard were executed at the Merkurea Cluk concentration camp, while another 32 were shot at Prahova. The newspapers reported that many other mass execution parties were also continuing at this time. The army had taken stern measures towards those who protested against authority. The guard on King Carol's palace was heavily reinforced, while soldiers patrolled all post offices and public buildings. At least 1,000 cavalrymen, armed with automatic weapons, arrived in Bucharest, while dispatches sent off to envoys abroad by the government stated that peace and order prevailed throughout Rumania, which would "remain strictly neutral during the war". However, Europe's neutral corner "trembled" over possible international repercussions following the assassination. The pro-German attitude of the Iron Guard was well known, and disturbing news reached Bucharest from Cernauti that the "German House" there had been raided by the police. They found material outlining the attitude to be adopted by German residents should their troops arrive on the frontier. Reports that the assassination had been plotted abroad were officially denied in Bucharest. But, in Paris, it was described as "the latest Nazi crime". The leader of the Iron Guard conspiracy, M Dumitrescu, who organized the crime, had recently returned from Prague, declared the Rumanian press. He had been in contact in Germany, it was stated, with groups of Iron Guard legionaries who had been waiting there for a year to make a "sensational" entry into the country.

Atrocities continued unabated throughout the Second World War. Polish women and children, along with 15,000 leaders, became the victims of German massacres in annexed western Poland. This news was declared by Polish diplomats in Rome on 2nd February 1940. In addition, 500,000 men and women were deported from the western provinces of Poznan, Pomerania and Upper Silesia, and thousands more were imprisoned in concentration camps under terrible conditions. Many prisoners and deportees were said to be dying of starvation. Embassies to both Italy and the Vatican declared that the Germans were seeking, through mass executions and deportations, to exterminate the Polish populations of the western provinces. The Associated Press reported that these accusations were contained in a pamphlet supplementing the one issued in late January 1939, which outlined mass persecutions in the same area. The document charged the Germans with shooting women and children without reason. A total of 50 people were publicly executed at Koscian, 15 at Gniezno and 16 at Kornik, said reports. The Germans also executed 136 students, some aged between 12 and 13, at Bydgoszcz. Similar public executions were reported at 15 other cities named in the report. It alleged that 300 out of 350 hostages arrested at Gdynia had been executed after being taken to Danzig and then to Wejherowe, where they had to dig their own graves before they were shot. "In Central Poland", the document said, "what is taking place is no less terrible". The report cited the alleged executions of five Poles in the marketplace at the provincial city of Szamotuly on 20th October after a Nazi flag was torn from the town hall. Five were reported to have been shot on the spot and others taken to Szamotuly to be shot publicly in the marketplace. "Many people shuddered with the horror of the scene and women fainted", stated the report. "After the execution several representatives of the intellectual class including a priest, a doctor and a lawyer, were ordered to load the bodies of their contemporaries on a wagon and take them to a nearby cemetery, where they were forced to dig the graves and bury the bodies."

Just a few months later, news reports were no better. On 25th March 1940, it was reported that while doctors and nurses stood in the courtyard of a Polish mental hospital, Gestapo agents slaughtered the 300 patients inside because they wanted the hospital as a headquarters for themselves, a Paris radio station announced. Assisted by members of the Iron Guard, the Nazis put a bullet into the head of every person in the building, including 40 orphan children who had been given refuge there. According to the reports of eyewitnesses, a similar mass murder took place just prior to the massacre at Owinska, near Posen, where 53 patients in a hospital for the mentally unsound were also put to death. Then, in mid-May 1940 it emerged that German troops in Poland were reported to have massacred 100 boy scouts, aged from 10 to 16, by lining them up against a wall and mowing them down with a machine gun. The incident occurred at Bydgoscz, and the news, which reached London on 15th May, was vouched for by the Boy Scouts Association. That same month, a road in northern France was choked with women and children refugees. Down each side of the road, six enemy tanks travelled, machine-gunning the women and children as they stood, and crushing all those who flung themselves to the ground in an attempt to avoid the bullets. The story, even by an eyewitness, was just one more piece of evidence of the ruthlessness with which the invading German hordes were carrying out massacres of helpless civilians.

In another incident, near Montreuil, an enemy plane was seen to break away from a formation of aircraft in order to attack a small party of refugees with bombs and machine-gun fire. King Leopold of Belgium was said to have informed President Roosevelt in the United States of the deliberate bombing by German planes of the American Hospital at Ostend. A French pilot was said to have reported the carnage, which according to the eyewitness involved German airmen dropping incendiary bombs on the building. Nearly all of the staff and patients perished in the incident.

In October 1941, while the Gestapo were hunting for victims in even the remotest villages of Czechoslovakia, thousands of people were hiding in the hills to escape their would-be executioners. Many were unable to stand the terror and torture. The number of suicides was appalling, according to Czech officials in London. At least 126 Czechs had been executed in the days leading up to early October, and hundreds more were waiting for the tragic farce of "trial" and an automatic sentence. To stop any food being hidden, the delivery of grain to mills had been forbidden after dark. From other parts of Europe enslaved by the Nazis came reports of attempted mass executions and increasing disorder as the spirit of the resistance grew. In Zagreb, two German soldiers were shot in the dark, and Montenegro and Southern Dalmatia were reported to be bordering on open revolt. In Bulgarian-occupied Macedonia, Greek people were reported to have attempted to revolt. In Hungarian-occupied Yugoslavia, 42 people were executed. A total of 15 Polish nationals were shot in public following the dynamiting of a bridge, and German troops at this time admitted to at least 1,000 executions in occupied countries since the invasion of Russia, according to the British United Press and the Associated Press. Later in October 1941, it was reported in a message sent to the Greek government that five German regiments had been sent into northern Greece to keep order. The Bulgarian authorities, to quell a rising in the districts of Drama Kavala and Kikne, immediately carried out instructions given by the German authorities to arrest all prominent people in the districts as hostages. During the night of 21st October several Bulgarians were killed in the suburbs of Kavala. Without any "trial" four hostages were executed for each Bulgarian alleged to have been killed. This and "other outrages" caused the revolt to spread all over the province of Drama, and a Bulgarian major sent out *agents provocateur* to foment minor disturbances. As a result, a series of brutal massacres was perpetrated, with statements by witnesses placing the number of victims at around 15,000. The village of Doxaton was turned into a heap of smoking ruins. Nevertheless, the Greek people put up a fight, despite being practically unarmed, and killed around 330 Bulgarians and seven German soldiers.

In the Russian town of Velizt, in the Smolensk region, German troops had arrested five Russians. They weren't fighters or guerrillas, but members of the civil population. All five were sentenced to hanging. On the outskirts of the town a gallows was built, and published pictures told the entire story of the executions. The photographs were found on a German officer killed on the Smolensk front. In a picture published in the *Daily Mirror* in February 1942, German soldiers were shown hanging from ropes. However, they were not being executed; the ropes were being tested for the hangings to come. The ropes tested, the five men then stood on a table under the gallows. Ropes were placed around their necks. In one picture, the man responsible for placing the ropes around the arrested men's necks is seen jumping from the table. Two men are poised at either end, ready to pull the table away. A fourth German soldier can be seen standing with a rifle ready to shoot any man that tried to make an escape. Stalin was quoted as saying: "Hitler wants a war of extermination – he shall have it. From now on, our task is to destroy, to exterminate these murderers."

Later that same month, on 24th February 1942, an article reported: "Frenchmen line up against a wall, singing and saluting their country. Bullets spit out from the German machine gun. The bodies… litter the ground." This was the version of the German troops' execution of French hostages given in *Liberation*, the secret newspaper distributed throughout occupied and unoccupied France at the risk of the lives of those who were behind it. Telling of the shooting of 50 people at Nantes, one of the eyewitness accounts said: "Among them were old men, cripples and heroes of the last war. Jost was there, President of the National Union of Communists. There were also youngsters, some of them almost children, like Noquais, son of the Paris deputy, just 17 years old. There was another 17-year-old there too." The witness continued: "The next day, thousands came with flowers and covered the bloodstained stones. These flowers are a pledge of revenge, a pledge that will be kept before long. A few days later, the Nantes Kommandatur published a list of 48 names. Forty-eight people murdered. Two names were missing and will not be revealed. The Germans are ashamed to admit – the two names were those of women." One German officer was known to have remarked that the 50 victims died with incredible courage, singing and saluting as they awaited the bullets that would take their lives. Meanwhile, at the concentration camp at Drancy, the saying went: "When they call us, it either means a shower bath, freedom, or death." *Liberation* said: "Above all this, there starts a whisper that swells and becomes a rumble and will one day develop into a roar... Meanwhile, we only say sons, brothers, wives and friends are keeping account. For every French life they have taken, we shall kill three of them."

In March 1942, 50 officers and men of the British army, prisoners of the Japanese, were bound hand and foot and bayoneted to death after the surrender of Hong Kong. Women, both European and Asiatic, were raped and murdered. One entire Chinese district was declared a brothel, regardless of the status of the inhabitants. The Japanese atrocities, "confirmed beyond any possibility of doubt", were disclosed in the House of Commons on 10th March by Anthony Eden, the Foreign Secretary. He promised that the atrocities would be given the widest possible publicity in all languages. Prefacing his disclosures by saying that the government was now in possession of statements from "reliable eyewitnesses" who escaped from Hong Kong, Eden said: "Their testimony establishes the fact that the Japanese army perpetrated against their helpless military prisoners and the civil population, without distinction of race or colour, the same kind of barbarities which aroused the horror of the civilized world at the time of the Nanking massacre of 1937. It is known that 50 officers and men of the British army were bound hand and foot and then bayoneted to death. It is known that 10 days after the capitulation wounded were still being collected from the hills and the Japanese were refusing permission to bury the dead.

"It is known that women, both Asiatic and European, were raped and murdered... All survivors of the garrison, including Indians, Chinese and Portuguese, have been herded into a camp consisting of wrecked huts, without doors, windows, light or sanitation. By the end of January, 150 cases of dysentery had occurred in the camp, but no drugs or medical facilities were supplied. The dead have to be buried in a corner of the camp. The Japanese guards are utterly callous and repeated requests by General Maltby, General Officer Commanding, for an interview with the Japanese commander have been curtly refused.

"This presumably means that the Japanese High Command have connived at the conduct of their forces. The Japanese government stated at the end of February that the number of prisoners in Hong Kong were: British 5,072, Canadian 1,659,

Indian, 3,829, others, 357... Most of the European residents, including some who are seriously ill, have been interned, but like the military prisoners are being given only a little rice and water, and occasional scraps of other food. Eden continued: "There is some reason to believe that the conditions have slightly improved recently, but the Japanese government have refused their consent to the visit to Hong Kong of representatives of the protecting Power, and no permission has yet been granted for such a visit by the International Red Cross Committee. They have, in fact, announced that they require all foreign consuls to withdraw from all the territories they have invaded since the outbreak of the war.

"It is clear that their treatment of prisoners and civilians will not bear independent investigation. I have no information as to the conditions of our prisoners of war and civilians in Malays. The only report available is a statement by the Japanese official news agency on March 3rd, which stated that 77,699 Chinese have been arrested and subjected to what is described as severe examination. It is not difficult to imagine what that entails. It is most painful to have to make such a statement to the House." Eden told the House of Commons that two things should be clear to the country, and the world. These were that the Japanese claim that their forces were animated by a lofty code of chivalry was obviously untrue and that they were therefore full of hypocrisy, and that the enemy must be defeated. Eden continued: "The House will agree with me that we can best express our sympathy with the victims of these appalling outrages by redoubling our efforts to ensure his utter and overwhelming defeat."

After hearing Eden's statement, Sir John Wardlaw-Milne, the Conservative MP for Kidderminster, asked if the Foreign Secretary would do everything possible to make the facts public so that the people of Britain would "at last know what they are up against and put their backs for once into the war". Eden replied that the only reason the government had not made a statement about the atrocities sooner was because they felt it would be wrong to do so unless absolutely convinced of the facts. Sir Percy Harris, Liberal MP for Bethnal Green, asked for it to be made clear that the Emperor, government and the whole of Japan were held responsible for the atrocities. Mr Lawson (Soc. Chester-le-Street), asked if special steps could be taken by the BBC to let the German and Italian people know how the Nazi "New Order" was working under their new ally. Eden confirmed that the "widest possible publicity in all languages will be given to these atrocities". He made it clear that the government did not consider the conditions of prisoners of war satisfactory. With the knowledge acquired following the Nanking massacre in 1937, feelings ran high. The former Chinese capital had fallen to the Japanese, where for two days after occupation there were wholesale lootings, attacks on women and murders of civilians. Japanese brutalities had been described by General Chiang Kai-Shek as "beyond description". When Nanking fell, more than 200,000 civilians were massacred within a week. It was well known that Japanese brutalities included rape, incendiarism and murder.

The full horror of the Japanese atrocities swept America along with the realization that Britons, Canadians and Americans were involved. Early reactions in America indicated that there was a nation-wide clamour for reprisals. A wave of anger also swept Canada, where the public was demanding that the authorities ceased "coddling" Japanese aliens. In Ottawa, Canadian sources recalled the statement on 15th February 1942 by Arnold Vaught, of the International Friends' Mission in Chungking, that 5,000 Hong Kong prisoners were living in an internment camp in Kowloon without proper food or sanitary facilities. He told how Empire troops begged for water as they marched past the Kowloon YMCA and how Japanese soldiers with bayonets drove away people who ran to give the prisoners water. The news of the atrocities shook the House of Commons probably more than anything that had happened up to this point in the war. Rumours of the atrocities had been circulating in the House for nearly a fortnight, but up to this point it was thought that the incidents had been exaggerated. Before the atrocities were made public, it was cited that Winston Churchill and President Roosevelt had had a number of conversations on the matter. The man more responsible than any other for instilling "the bestiality into the Japanese soldier", was General Hideki Tojo, the Japanese Prime Minister. Known as "The Razor", he was responsible for the blockade of Tientsin four years earlier, where Britons were stripped and humiliated.

In Europe, the treatment of prisoners of war received significant press attention. "Unless the German government release the prisoners captured at Dieppe from their chains, an equal number of German prisoners of war will be manacled as from noon tomorrow," read the *Daily Mirror* on 9th October 1942. The War Office announcement followed a declaration the day before by a German radio commentator that British men had been put in chains. Earlier in the day, the British and Canadian governments had been in "urgent consultation". An earlier British government statement, after pointing out that the German government's reprisals were forbidden by Article 2 of the Geneva Convention, had hinted that similar measures would be taken against enemy prisoners in British hands. The statement repeated the declaration, made in reply to the Nazis' excuse that they were acting in reprisal for the tying of Germans captured in the Sark raid (Operation *Basalt*), that the British government did not and would not countenance any orders for tying the hands of prisoners.

The announcement that the Dieppe men had been put in chains was made by a radio commentator, who seized the opportunity to try to deride the Allied warning that Axis war criminals would be punished. "Take heed lest Germany should one day adopt this decision for its own purposes and apply it to Mr Roosevelt and other Allied warmongers", he said. "In one respect this has been already done." Since noon on 9th October, British prisoners had been put in chains as a retaliation for similar crimes committed by the British. London had given an explanation, though it was a war crime against German honour according to newspaper reports. The BBC broadcast the news of Britain's reprisals to Germany and repeated forcibly the government's warning that there were 170,000 more German and Italian prisoners in British hands than there were British prisoners in Germany and Italy. The government's reply to the German allegations was a reminder that if the Nazis chained British men they did so at their peril.

In other news, escaping from a Nazi prison camp in France, two British soldiers reported missing after Dunkirk walked 1,600 miles in bitter weather through Belgium, Holland, Germany and Poland to reach safety in Russia. Most of the time they were dodging Nazis and for long spells they lived on berries, mushrooms and grass, along with anything else they could forage from woods and fields. Two others that joined them in the escape were lost on the journey. It was not known whether they died of exposure or were shot by German troops. It was only when a Russian national arrived in the UK and called at the London home of the parents of one of the men that they heard their son, Sergeant Louis Massey, was alive and safe. He was said to be working at the British Embassy in Moscow, and was subsequently awarded the DCM.

In December 1942, the Archbishop of York, Cyril Garbett, made an important speech in Parliament in which he demanded full retribution, not only against Nazi leaders, but against their thousands of "underlings savaging occupied Europe". His bold attack seemed to signal the emergence of a statesman. In his declaration, he echoed the sober judgment of the "common man". The Archbishop was speaking in the House of Lords in a debate opened by Lord Strabolgi on the measures to be taken to relieve distress in Europe when the subjugated countries were freed from German occupation. Agreeing on the necessity for making plans, the Archbishop called for stern retribution against those responsible for the pitiable condition of the people in occupied France. "If the war goes on there is the possibility that one nation, at any rate, may be exterminated", he said. "We know there are multitudes of people starving in Greece, but at the moment in Poland there is taking place one of the most appalling outrages the whole history of the world has ever seen. We are watching the deliberate and cold-blooded massacre of a nation. The extermination of all the Jews in that country has been decided upon and will be carried out ruthlessly." He continued: "Men, women and children are ruthlessly put to death by massacre, poison gas, electrocution and by being sent on long journeys to unknown destinations in bitterly cold weather without food and drink. Children are cast from trucks to the side of the railway. It is almost impossible to know what can be done when we are dealing with such monsters of iniquity who are ordering these cruelties."

In his call to the Lords to prepare a post-war plan of aid for Europe, Lord Strabolgi declared: "You have a great strategic weapon, if you can convince the nations now groaning under the Nazi yoke that when their oppressors are driven out of their countries they will immediately receive help in restoring their industries." Lord Wedgwood said he wondered who was going to pay for post-war assistance and who was going to find the raw materials. "They are not coming from us", he said. "We are one of the chief suppliants for assistance." Lord Maugham said the first thing to be done was to take from Germany all the articles that the country had robbed the conquered countries of, and return them to their owners. Viscount Cranborne, replying to the debate, said the Allied Committee set up to prepare estimates of post-war requirements of European Allied countries had made good progress. Provisional estimates had been received from all the Allied governments with regard to their requirements of foodstuffs during the first 18 months after the war, and most of them had submitted lists of medical requirements and provided estimates for all or most of the important classes of raw materials and industrial goods. Meanwhile, Slovakia was warned that nationals aiding the Nazi persecution of the Jews would be put to death. Masaryk, the Czechoslovakian foreign minister, said in a broadcast to his country: "Hitler's anti-Jewish madness grows in proportion with the imminence of his defeat."

By February 1943, it was reported that 6,000 Jews were being killed every day in one area of Poland alone. The Nazi authorities had issued new orders to speed up and intensify the extermination by massacre and starvation of the Jews remaining in Occupied Europe. Reports to this effect from Central Europe were received in London by the British section of the World Jewish

Congress. Before being massacred, the Jews were ordered to strip, and their clothes were then sent to Germany. The Nazis decreed that by 31st March 1942 the "Protectorate" of Bohemia and Moravia was to be cleared of Jews and that by the same date no Jew was to be left in Berlin. An order virtually sentencing the Jews of Bohemia and Moravia to death by starvation was published in the official gazette of the Protectorate. Under this decree, local authorities were ordered to withdraw cards for rationed foodstuffs from Jews. Under the existing regulations, Jews were also forbidden to buy unrationed foodstuffs, such as fish, poultry and vegetables. At the same time, deportations of Jews from Germany were continuing rapidly and special Gestapo agents from Vienna, where deportations had almost been completed, had been sent to Holland to speed up the expulsions. Even young women working in German war industries whose parents had already been deported were arrested and deported too. Not a single Jew was left in the ghetto of Warsaw according to the *Daily Mirror*, where before the mass extermination began there were once 430,000. There were just 55 Jewish ghettos remaining in Poland at the beginning of 1943. A special report from Rumania stated that 130,000 Jews were deported in the autumn of 1941 to Transnistria. Meanwhile, it emerged from the US Office of War Information that Warsaw was being made into a Nazi testing-ground for the ruthless extermination of Allied populations. A statement, issued in New York, said that Germany were trying to eliminate Warsaw by means of outright murder and the encouragement of disease and starvation, and that there was ample evidence of the city "dying out". Children in Warsaw were "malformed and ghostlike", suffering from anemia and softening of the bones. A couple of months later, in April 1943, the Polish government issued an official statement that gave no indication of its being prepared to withdraw its demand for an inquiry into Germany's massacre of Polish officers. Instead, it made a "sensational" plea for the release from Russia of the families of all Polish servicemen fighting with the United Nations. There were tens of thousands of Polish orphans that were considered "particularly precious" to the Polish people. That same month, Japanese troops slaughtered every man, woman and child in the coastal areas of China where American aircraft had landed after bombing Tokyo. The news was revealed by the Secretary of the US Treasury, Henry Morgenthau, Jr, who said that a cablegram from General Chiang Kai-Shek had declared: "After they had been caught unawares by the falling of bombs on Tokyo, the Japanese troops attacked the coastal areas of China and slaughtered every man, woman and child in those areas, reproducing on a large scale, horrors which the world had seen at Lidice. The only language such an enemy understands is that of war."

It was later reported that around 500,000 people had been massacred by the Japanese. The Reverend Vincent Smith, a missionary in China who was one of the few survivors of the coastal attacks said: "Whole towns of 15,000 to 20,000 people were wiped out... This was the fate of 30 or 40 towns of this size in 400 miles of the province. Only a handful of people who fled to the hills were not sighted and survived." In August 1943, the word on everyone's lips was punishment.

After the First World War, in the aftermath of victory, there had been much talk of punishing of war criminals. "Hang the Kaiser", was then a popular sentiment. It was both a slogan and a song. The *Daily Mirror* wrote: "Probably the general opinion, in these days, would be that we should have gained nothing by beheading or hanging, on Tower Hill or in Trafalgar Square, a man who was perhaps rather crazy than criminal." As signs of victory in the Second World War grew on the horizon, the question of what to do with war criminals was raised. The *Daily Mirror* declared that war criminals would find it more difficult than their "forerunners and counterparts" did in 1918. It said: "There are so few neutral retreats for human brutes." The President of the United States had given his word and "set his face against the artful dodgers" who were already planning a good getaway. Even men like Franco it was believed would find war criminals to be "awkward guests". The paper stated: "It is not unlikely that, after our victory, there will be no Franco. As the peoples everywhere recover their rights and rise in righteous indignation they will know how to deal with those who sat on dirty fences." The article continued: "This is indeed an important point – leave punishment, if punishment there is to be, to the peoples who have suffered so bitterly. There is always the risk that a spectacular Allied Tribunal, composed of eminent Judges assembled from a score of countries, may, as they spin cobwebs of international law, confer a sort of dignity upon the war criminals. With a good deal of ingenuity, based on much secret support from those who still have a sneaking liking for Dictators, who make the trains run to time, it might be possible to turn even murderers like Mussolini into martyrs. Certainly, it will be possible in Germany."

The article stated how, at the end of the Great War, the Allies had made the mistake of negotiating armistice and peace with "phantoms who ever afterwards took the blame that really belonged to the German military caste." Hitler was therefore able to tell his take about traitors and "their stab in the back". It should, the paper argued, be made plain to all the world that the war criminals had tried to wade through "rivers of blood" to world power, and that they "hideously, catastrophically, failed". Punishment, it was felt, should follow. However, the Nazis were not the only extermination experts. In August 1943 it emerged that the Italians were also "quite expert and brutal" with regard to extermination. More than 100,000 Yugoslavs were herded into concentration camps by the Italians, and one particularly horrific account came from the camp on the island of Rab, in the Adriatic. People sent there were "inevitably doomed to death". More than 14,000 people, including women and children, were interned in the winter of 1942 in a swampy encampment where tents were the only protection against the fierce Adriatic storms. Every day during that winter between 40 and 60 people died, and a further 3,000 were known to have perished from famine or disease.

"A cemetery of living skeletons", was the phrase used in one report to describe the people herded to Rab. "People who have left the terrible island of Rab have been taken to another camp at Gonars – whose death rate is 10 to 12 a day", said another. One report even went so far as to say: "If it is desired to let these people die, it would be advisable to hasten the procedure." One Italian officer reported that 60 out of every 100 people would die if they did not get more food. The Italian authorities prevented the organization of any relief for the camp internees on the grounds that Yugoslavia no longer existed. Whole populations were transferred to foreign countries and exposed to terrible hardships. On one list alone, some 80 concentration camps were planned for Yugoslav nationals.

The Archbishop of York was back in the news in December 1943 when he declared that Nazi atrocities had been proved by "irresistible evidence", and supported the demand for legal vengeance on war criminals. Speaking in the House of Lords, he said that Nazi cruelty and wholesale slaughter had been unique in the way in which it had been almost solely concentrated against people who were helpless and harmless, and indiscriminately against men, women and children. He said that the evidence came from country after country and was overwhelming. He continued: "We want to get at the men who have corrupted and perverted the youth and manhood of Germany and who are responsible for these crimes. If Hitler and Himmler managed to escape to a neutral country while their subordinates suffered at home, it would be a monstrous outrage against justice." Lord Simon, replying for the government, said: "There must be no mass executions merely because there have been mass executions on the other side. We shall never do any good if what we do is not consistent with justice. Do not let us wait until the peace treaty is signed before we insist on the surrender of those whom we wish to accuse of war crimes." He then warned neutral countries: "There is no such thing in international law as a right of asylum attaching to an individual. It does not give to the refugee any right to say, 'Here I am and here I will stay'."

On 18th December 1943, it was reported that SS Lieutenant Hans Ritz, 24, a self-confessed tommy-gun murderer of 300 Russian men, women and children, loved to send photographs of himself beside hanged Partisans to his fiancée, "in order to conquer her sentimental heart". This revelation of the warped mentality of a peacetime lawyer turned wartime killer was given in the Moscow newspaper *Izvestia*. The small man, "with a birdlike and childish face", was one of four accused in the Kharkov atrocities trial. He put all the blame on Hitler, whom he named as "war criminal No.1", with Himmler and Rosenberg coming second and third. Asked who was actually responsible for the system of "complete lawlessness and monstrous cruelty", on the Eastern Front, Ritz replied: "This lawlessness has its deep reasons. It was established on the instructions of Hitler and his collaborators. The chief culprit is Hitler who calls for a system of cruelty and speaks of the superiority of the German-Aryan race, which is called upon to establish order in Europe." Himmler had stated repeatedly that there was no need to pay any attention to the paragraphs entailing the death sentence, but that the death sentence had to be imposed according to "one's Aryan instinct". Ritz admitted that between 5th June and 1st September 1943, the people shot in Taganrog and its neighbourhood numbered around 3,000. He said: "During a visit to Kharkov I met Major Hannebecker, who told me they were about to execute 3,000 citizens who had expressed excessive joy when the town was occupied by Soviet troops."

On 9th January 1944, General "Lightning" Vatutin announced another Red army offensive. "Local breaches" in grim fighting in an ice-covered country 100 miles north of the Kiev bridge were reported. Powerful infantry forces were said to have led the attack, which was launched on a broad front along the railway west of Rechitsa, in the Gomel region, after a heavy artillery barrage. Vatutin's troops had surged six miles across the former border after uprooting the yellow-and-black frontier posts marked "Deutschland". Reports said that German losses everywhere on both the First and Second Ukrainian fronts were considerable, and in some sectors resembled a massacre. Prior to this, according to Moscow radio, thousands of inhabitants of Kirovograd had been shot dead during the German occupation. It was stated that: "Five thousand citizens, including boys little over 10 years of age were lined up, marched to the outskirts of the town and shot with tommy-guns. Those who were not killed outright were buried alive." Before retreating, German troops killed about 10,000 Russian prisoners of war in a camp just outside the town and drove thousands of "peasants" away.

On 26th January 1944, Stalin issued a report proving that German troops had massacred at least 11,000 Polish prisoners at Katyn, near Smolensk, and then faked their burial to make it appear that Russians had committed the atrocity. Duncan Hooper of Reuters, who went with a party of Allied journalists to watch the Soviet Commission investigating the massacre, sent a grim story back to the UK:

"From the top of a mound we looked down into a huge pit where, packed like sardines, were layers of bodies of Polish officers and men. It was as if a section of a football crowd had been lifted up bodily and pressed into the earth. The shrunken figures looked like rag dolls. Red army men in rubber gloves were working in the grave, prising out the bodies for examination. Our guide was Professor Victor Prozorovsky, director of a Moscow medical research institute, who told us that more than 700 bodies had been taken from seven graves.

"The dead are officially estimated at 11,000, but the professor himself thinks that when all the graves are opened the number will be found to be between 12,000 and 15,000. Eleven teams of surgeons and their assistants, dealing with about 160 bodies a day, are carrying out post-mortem examinations from dawn to dusk. All the bodies had been shot through the back of the head at close range. Some had their hands tied behind their backs.

I watch Professor Prozorovsky carry out a post-mortem. As he deftly removed the brain, he told me that all the bodies had been buried for about two years."

The German army had occupied Smolensk in July 1941. When they tried in the spring of 1943 to place responsibility on Russian troops, creating friction between Moscow and the exiled Polish government, German authorities alleged that the executions had taken place in 1940. Hooper continued: "I saw an unposted card dated June 29, 1941, which had been found on one of the bodies. Stanislaus Korhinsky had written to his wife Irena in Warsaw: 'Dear Little Sunbeam – We must not forget each other. Remember you are all I possess. I want you to sell all my things so that you can look after yourself and eat properly, darling.'" Hooper confirmed that Potemkin, Commissar for Education, told him the Commission was satisfied that the German troops took the Polish men from their camps, rounded up others from the countryside and shot them all secretly in groups behind barbed wire in the Katyn Forest. The German execution unit was known as the "537th Construction Battalion", with its headquarters in a former rest home in the Forest. In the spring of 1943 about 500 Red army prisoners, who were afterwards shot, were forced to exhume the bodies and remove all compromising documents. Civilians, beaten with rubber whips, were forced to sign faked evidence.

The news that the German High Commission was deliberately spreading typhus amongst Russian nationals was broadcast by

Moscow radio on 1st May 1944. Many German generals were linked in the "new atrocity" revelations, which quoted a great fund of evidence of more mass killings and other merciless brutalities practised by the German army on helpless Soviet citizens. Declaring that all those responsible would have to pay a severe penalty for their crimes, the Moscow statement said: "It has been established that by creating concentration camps in forward areas and by placing in them healthy people together with people infected with typhus, the German military authorities attempted to spread the typhus epidemic among the Soviet people and the Red army." One infected woman told the Russian Commission of Inquiry that German soldiers forced her to move to a camp in order to infect as many people as possible. There were many other similar stories. As a result, many healthy people in camps fell sick and began to die of the disease. To make matters worse, the inquiry found that the camps consisted of open spaces surrounded by barbed wire, and that approaches were mined. There were no buildings nor any kind of lighting. In March 1944 the advancing Red army discovered three concentration camps like this. The camps housed more than 33,000 children, disabled women and elderly people. "Those in the camps had to lie on the ground. Some unable to move any longer, were lying deep in mud," the inquiry was told. "The inmates were forbidden to light fires or to gather brushwood for bedding. The Nazis shot any who made the slightest attempt to break this order. On the way to the camps the Germans picked out all the able-bodied men, women and children over 13 years of age, and sent them to forced labour in Germany. The remainder, including the younger children, were sent to the camps.

"Many children froze and died of the cold and hunger in the wagons. Many old people and women also died." One man said that beside the barbed wire with which the camp was surrounded were ditches filled with dirty marsh water. Many decomposing bodies lay in the ditches. "The Germans gave us no water to drink and we were forced to drink from those ditches", the man said.

Also in May 1944, the British government made inquiries through Switzerland, as protecting power, regarding Stockholm reports that 2,700 Allied prisoners of war, including 53 British, had died in suspicious circumstances in an unregistered prisoner-of-war camp near Bremen. The reports also said that 27 British and Dominion prisoners had been shot at Graudenz, on the river Vistula. There was no confirmation of the reports at the time, but they were considered so serious that the British government considered it necessary to make an official inquiry. Lord Vansittart told the House of Lords on 15th May that the personnel at Stalag Luft III, the camp where 47 shot British officers had been imprisoned, should be tried after the war. The slaughter of the 47 officers was, he declared, "murder and nothing else". He said: "We all know the old German pretext of shooting while attempting flight. That formula was in use for many years before the war. It is… the most flimsy pretext for massacre." Lord Vansittart said it was quite impossible for 47 men to have been shot dead without any being wounded. "I think they were lined up and mown down. The executioner operated at close quarters and made no mistake." Speaking for the government, Lord Cranborne said: "It must be our object to ensure that those responsible for this odious and brutal crime shall be held responsible for it."

A French girl of 18, lying in a Normandy hospital with a shattered leg, told a war correspondent on 2nd July 1944 a story of German brutality to civilians caught up in fighting after the Allied landings in Normandy. The young woman, a saleswoman in a Caen shop, said: "Your planes bombed Caen on the afternoon of June 6. We went to a farm… all night your shells were bursting round us. Next day my mother, my 10-year-old sister and myself followed the farmer, his wife and his three young children and crouched in a slit trench 100 yards from the house covered with faggots. There was also a young peasant of 20 there. An hour after I heard German voices. There were four or five of them, all very young. One pulled up the faggots and told us to come out.

"I was terrified. The farmer's wife called out 'Don't shoot' but he fired four times. The first bullet killed the babies' father. The second killed the young peasant. The third shot a two-year-old child through the leg. The fourth smashed my leg. I was suffering horribly, but made myself a bandage. Everyone was crying, and we passed the night in the trench with two corpses. After hours of nightmare, civilians came and carried me on a ladder to a British hospital where I was well cared for." The young woman told the war correspondent that she believed that if instructed, the German army would shoot to kill, but until that point, she had never believed they would shoot people for the sake of it, especially helpless women and children. However, that same month worse was to follow with a massacre of French men, women and children by SS troops in northern France that surpassed even the horror of Lidice. The disclosure came from the French Provisional government in Algiers that the mass murder came about in the village of Oradour sur Glane, in the Vienne department. Just seven people out of around 800 survived. The massacre was carried out by SS troops as a possible reprisal for the killing of German soldiers, or perhaps because an arms depot was found in the town. Without warning, the entire population was hustled into the village square. Then, while the women and children wept and prayed for mercy, their men were dragged off to a nearby shed in groups of 20 and shot down with machine-gun fire. With their children clinging to their skirts, the women were driven into the church of Oradour sur Glane and locked inside with a large case of high explosives. An hour later, the SS troops set fire to the village. The flames soon began to flicker around the church. The screaming inside the church only stopped as the ammunition exploded and the building crashed down around those inside. Some of the women and children, however, survived so the troops waited until they tried to flee the burning buildings and then shot anyone they saw. On the same day this news was reported, the British government gave a pledge in the House of Lords that the Gestapo would be made to pay for their crimes. It was suggested that the entire Gestapo – 200,000 men together with all volunteers – should be outlawed.

On 20th July 1944, Bill Greig wrote in the *Daily Mirror* that an attempt had been made by the German government to get war supplies in exchange for the lives of Jews in Hungary. The British government had refused to bargain with the lives of men, women and children, and both Russia and America had been in complete agreement. Greig published the full extent of the blackmail as one of the most extraordinary incidents of the war, which he claimed would go down in history. At various times in the months leading up to July 1944, there had been indirect hints from German agents abroad that Germany might be persuaded to change its attitude towards the Jews in return for some unnamed concessions. Then came news of a massacre of Jews in Hungary, which caused an outcry of indignation and anger throughout the world. It was reliably reported that 100,000 Jewish people had been taken to Poland and gassed. Almost immediately afterwards, two men identified as representatives of the Gestapo arrived in a neutral capital, and through diplomatic channels suggested that a deal might be made with regard to the lives of those who survived. They suggested that if the Allies would agree to supply Germany with certain war materials there would be no more executions, and in addition, the Nazi policy towards the Jewish people would be considered modified.

The goods required were forms of transport, principally rail and road trucks, and they suggested that these could be supplied from stocks in the Middle East. At the same time, Jewish leaders were approached about the proposals. At all times, the Gestapo representatives tried to take the line that they were acting on their own responsibility from purely humanitarian motives and not representing the German government. There was no doubt, however, in official circles that an attempt was being made by the Nazis to discover how far the Allies could be blackmailed in an attempt to save lives. From unofficial but reliable sources, it emerged that the number of people already sent to face death in the gas chambers were a staggering 400,000.

However, by 25th July 1944 it was apparent that Himmler had started a new blood purge that far eclipsed the massacre of 30th June 1934. General Oberst Josef Dietrich, who had followed Hitler since the beginning of his career, was listed by the Russians as a war criminal because of his atrocities at Kharkoff. He was the commander of the SS Panzer Corps, and the most trusted of all Nazi generals. Dietrich was Hitler's personal watch dog until the Führer was firmly in power, and as a reward was given high military rank. His meteoric rise never attracted much attention outside Germany, probably because militarily he achieved practically nothing except promotion. His presence in Normandy in 1944, however, was cited as probably of more importance to Hitler personally than that of Rommel. Dietrich commanded the core of German resistance in Normandy, and could not afford to let Hitler down. There was little news of further individuals until December 1944 when five of the six German war criminals found guilty of taking part in the mass murders in the extermination camp at Majdanek in Poland were sentenced to death by a Polish court in London. They were to be hanged in public. The sixth war criminal hanged himself in his cell during the trial, having anticipated that he would be found guilty. But the hanging of five guilty men and the suicide of another did not deter the German authorities. On 21st December 1944 it was reported that the German army were murdering Americans they had captured in the Battle of the Bulge. The news about the atrocities was confirmed by First army HQ reporting to Washington.

In one incident, German tanks turned their guns on and wiped out 125 US artillerymen and medical personnel who had surrendered in the area of Monschau. A total of 15 soldiers – all of them wounded – managed to escape. One said: "On December 17, our field artillery battery encountered German tanks on a road and were also fired at from the sides of the road. We sought cover but were ultimately taken prisoner. The men, some 140 of them, were robbed of their cigarettes and valuables and then ordered into a field with their hands up. Suddenly a single shot was fired at us, then tank machine-guns opened up, firing at all of us lying prostrate. The shooting continued until a pile of dead and wounded were lying on the ground. I and other men feigned death and during a lull ran into a wood."

Another eyewitness account said that only a few miles from the scene of the first atrocity, a second ruthless slaying of helpless prisoners had taken place under equally shocking conditions. A

Nazi officer had ordered the prisoners to be taken to an open field where, after being searched, they were told to hold their hands above their heads. Suddenly, tank machine guns poured lead up and down their lines until all were lying on the ground. Then the bloody, screaming mass of American soldiers lying on the ground were shot by individual German troops seeking to make sure that their fate was sealed. This report was cabled by Reuters correspondent John Wilhelm. An American broadcast from Belgium on 20th December described the situation in one area as "grave". Numbers of US troops had been cut off near St Vith, 10 miles south of Malmedy, and seven miles inside Belgium. "Our troops are caught in the German armoured pincers which have now carried the enemy to a point within three miles of St Vith" the broadcast claimed. Meanwhile, the German drive into Belgium with armour, infantry and parachute troops had seen four main thrusts.

By early the following year, in February 1945, the United States feared that Ireland would become a possible hideout for Nazi war criminals. Prospects for Nazi war criminals being able to obtain secure haven in neutral countries after the war looked extremely "bright" according to British and American experts on international law. The experts were urgently warning their governments that unless a firmer stand was made with neutral nations, the task of arresting and trying the criminals would be rather hopeless. The US government was giving the problem increasing attention, but the British government seemed, to reporters at least, to still be relying on vague "assurances" given by several neutral nations. The US State Department was worried most by the possibility that Ireland would become the chief haven, and second and third on the list were Portugal and Spain. Portugal had already rebuffed suggestions from Italy's Bonomi administration for the Fascist war criminal, Count Dino Grandi, to be extradited. The Allies had also received no convincing assurances from Argentina with regard to the granting of asylum to Nazis. Meanwhile, Germany was known to have accumulated large stocks of foreign passports, confiscated from citizens in the countries they overran. These could easily be altered for use by escaping Nazis, for the Gestapo and other agencies had large staffs of expert forgers. Once on neutral soil, it would present an extremely difficult situation for those seeking their extradition under what was then international law.

"Murderer, war criminal, confidence trickster and coward" wrote the *Daily Mirror* on 23rd February 1945. "Count Dino Grandi has reminded us he is still at large by a belated attempt to whitewash himself in interviews."

"Are we scared of this war criminal?" the paper asked. The wanted man, who was Mussolini's Ambassador in London for seven years, had shaved off his beard, adopted the name of Dominico Galli, and settled with his wife and family in sunny Estoril in Portugal. For one war criminal at least, US fears had been proved true. Badoglio quietly gave him a passport in recognition of the fact that when Italy collapsed he voted against

Mussolini on the Fascist Grand Council. Grandi was, therefore, able to escape from his country while some of his former criminal cronies were being arrested and brought to trial. In June 1944 the Italian government invited Grandi to return home and face charges of taking part in the inauguration and leadership of the Fascist movement. But he was too cowardly to accept. There were several charges of murder against him, dating as far back as the early 1920s when he led expeditions against peasants who dared oppose Fascism. There were those who asked why the British government was permitting this notorious war criminal to remain at large, who wondered if Britain was scared of asking Portugal to extradite Grandi. There were others who asked if he was being protected by the influence of British politicians who had been charmed by his exquisite social graces, pretty wife and winsome children during his years as an ambassador in London. Wickham Steed described him as a "murderous villain" who, along with Mussolini, brought about a movement that spread to Germany and Japan and encouraged war and millions of deaths across the globe.

In 1922, Grandi had joined his fellow "gangster" in the March on Rome. Then, with a mob of thugs, he set about imposing Fascism by force. He was said to have boasted that he shot down 30 men with his own gun in Bologna, but Grandi was not so much of a fighter as he was a smooth and cunning confidence trickster. This was why Mussolini appointed him as ambassador to Britain in 1932, after he had received sound training in undercover work as foreign minister. His job was to fool the British government and people with a pretence of friendship, while Mussolini secretly prepared Italy for the inevitable war against world democracy. "I am convinced", he purred when he reached Britain, "that Britain and Italy will travel the same road hand in hand working for peace, progress and the welfare of humanity". While in Britain, he flattered his way into friendships, particularly among elderly Tories and Mayfair hostesses. He and his wife would hold big parties – on one occasion 2,000 invites were sent out – and he was cleverly photographed playing with his children or petting a cute dog. He was described in the wealthy circles of Mayfair as having "such a charming family", but as time passed Mussolini's warlike intentions became increasingly obvious. Grandi, for his part, smoothed down elderly politicians with grace. As Ethiopia was invaded and Italy went to the aid of Franco in Spain, Grandi continued to hold lavish parties in London so that he could assure the British government and others besides that Mussolini loved peace. Meanwhile, there were Britons that "toadied" to Grandi in the hope that Italy would not be unkind. An "Anglo-Italian" group formed by Conservative MPs gave him dinners and invited Lord Halifax, the Foreign Secretary, along to mingle and network. Newspapers noted afterwards that Grandi must have chuckled. At the same time, German and Italian plans for war had progressed so far by May 1939 that Grandi was able to drop his mask and speak his mind. In a speech at the Italian Embassy, he violently attacked Britain and France, and sneered at their "furious impotence". Praising the alliance between Italy and Germany, he predicted it would produce "just peace for the two great Fascist nations, a new cycle of greater and more dazzling victories". The speech caused a sensation with Churchill, Eden and Attlee, turning them "green with bile". After his work was done, Grandi was recalled to Italy, where he shouted: "The command today is absolute fidelity to you, O Duce; blind faith in the paths you trace out for us; silent, virile obedience to your orders." In April 1940 he warned: "Italy can no longer stand outside the conflict." In 1945, having successfully moved on and found a life of comfort he sat in interviews and told anyone willing to listen "what a fine fellow" he was.

In April 1945, German military authorities in western Holland broadcast a rejection of what they called General Eisenhower's "proposal" that food should be flown by the Allies to the starving population of Nazi-occupied Holland. However, Eisenhower did not ask for permission; he said the planes would be coming and that any interference with them would be punished as a war crime. On 25th April, German authorities said the planes would be used to conduct reconnaissance of their defences, and that the food might get into the hands of black marketeers. They argued that the food should be sent via land and sea. However, that would mean the food passing through German hands, and as the British United Press pointed out, Germany was running short of food. A Reuters correspondent cabled that unless food was sent to the Dutch immediately – and nothing but air transport would be quick enough – there would be a tragedy overshadowing even that of Buchenwald and Belsen. The daily death rate from starvation in the two months prior was 400 in The Hague and between 500 and 600 in Amsterdam. For six months food rations had been far below the level needed to sustain life.

"Horror camp report" read the headline in the *Daily Mirror* on 28th April 1945. The report of the parliamentary delegation to the Buchenwald camp, published the day before, described a scene of "intense general squalor, the odour of dissolution and disease pervading the entire place". One hut had been used as a brothel for the "higher grade" prisoners. In general, the camp was for men and boys only. "The women in this brothel" said the report, "were prisoners from other camps induced by threats and promises of better treatment to become prostitutes, but subsequently killed". The worst cases of malnutrition were unable to speak and lay in a "semi-coma". All prisoners were in an extreme state of emaciation. Members of Parliament were told by the US authorities that since their arrival, deaths had been reduced from about 100 a day before the delegation's visit to 35. "One half-naked skeleton, tottering painfully along the passage as though on stilts, drew himself up when he saw the party", the report said. Medical members of the delegation expressed the opinion that a percentage of the prisoners could not be expected to survive even with the treatment they were receiving, and that a larger percentage, though they might survive, would probably suffer sickness and disablement for the rest of their lives. Some of the men had undergone operations by prison doctors performed without anaesthetics on a crude operating table at one end of the hut in full view of other patients. There were no mattresses. "If the living were strong enough, they pushed the dead out into the gangway. Each night the dead were thrown into a small annex at one end of the hut and each morning collected and taken in carts to the crematorium or as specimens to the pathological laboratory of the Nazi doctors." Children, like adults, were made to work eight or more hours a day, seven days a week. One 14-year-old boy from Poland stated he had seen his 18-year-old brother shot dead and his parents taken away for what he believed to be cremation. He never saw them again. There was also a "mortuary block" where access to the basement was by a steep stone staircase or by a vertical chute below a trap door. "Hanging appears to have been the regular method of killing", the report stated. "In the yard near a pile of white ashes, there was a gibbet, in the basement we saw strong hooks at a height of about eight feet from the floor and another gibbet. We were informed that there had been more than 40 hooks, most of which the Nazis had removed hurriedly before leaving. We were shown a heavy wooden club about 2ft long... it was stained with blood." The report continued: "Bodies were transported from this basement to the ground floor crematorium in a large electric lift similar to those used for stretcher cases in hospitals. To the yard outside the crematorium came the carts, packed closely with the ordinary corpses from the dysentery and other huts, mostly stripped even of the meager striped blue and white suits which were the normal camp clothing." At the same time, the "Women of Mercy" arrived in Belsen's torture camp, where seven were members of a Friends Service unit, and others were members of Red Cross units. Doctors and nurses had been clearing up the "dreadful human debris" in Belsen and attempting to save those they could. The work of the mercy mission, however, was to get administration going as soon as possible, lay down water systems, classify the survivors and make sure that all epidemics were wiped out. Their other work involved moving all survivors to hospitals within a reasonable distance. The worst part of the job was deciding who could make it as a survivor and who was too sick to be saved. The mercy mission also had responsibility for saving the minds of the camp survivors who had been brutalized for many years. It was the job of the Women of Mercy to bring these people back to some kind of normality. They needed to be taught that food was there as a given right, and not "as a fresh torture". They needed to be washed and clothed. It was a painstaking task.

Also in the news at the time was the fact that the German authorities were trying to slow down the Red army's progress in Berlin by using another war crime – the use of Soviet citizens as hostages in their buildings. In spite of these tactics, the Red army continued its task of clearing key areas. One Soviet group advanced a distance of nearly three miles overnight and broke into the Moabit district adjoining the Tiergarten. By this time the capital had become a "city of horror" for its surviving population, with "civilians waiting numbly for the end". There were almost no buildings left in which to place the wounded in what had become, "a stony desert... with flames of burning streets... heavily charged with brick and cement dust".

On 11th May 1945, Herbert Pell, a former member of the War Crimes Commission, told a New York audience that: "Goering and other Nazi criminals are surrendering to the Americans because they are confident nothing will happen to them." It was even reported that: "Official representatives of this [US] government have shaken hands and sat down to dinner with Goering, this monstrous and perverted being who treacherously unloosed a ruthless air power upon undefended cities and peoples." On 17th May that year, Lieutenant-General Lucius Clay, Deputy Military Governor in Germany for General Eisenhower, declared that Doenitz, Goering, Kesselring, Rundstedt and other Nazi chiefs were being moved to "selected places of incarceration" where they would remain as ordinary prisoners of war until they could be tried. But Robert Murphy, US member of the Allied Control Commission, said Doenitz was recognized as representing the German high command. Clay stated that he hoped the trials would "be soon" and said: "German war criminals will pay for their crimes with their lives, liberty, seat and blood. The punishment of war criminals is our first objective." Nazis that joined the party before 1933 would be thrown out of influential jobs by the new military-ruled government, overseen by the US, and would be offered work digging ditches or graves. The Allies had arrested "Back-room Nazis", including bankers and industrialists, and many others were under restraint. It was declared that all would be tried as war criminals.

Up until 3rd July 1945, a German-run "death hospital" continued its "work" of killing off women and children in Kaufbeuren, Bavaria. The little town housed one of the infamous "extermination factories" operating under the guise of an institution, but the "horrible" facts were hidden until the US army arrived. The Nazis at the hospital had labelled "inmates" as "mental" or "cripple" cases in defiance of surrender laws and continued with their heinous work. Death came through injections or starvation and the chief nurse confessed to the murder of more than 200 children in two years. Another nurse admitted poisoning at least 40 people.

On 4th August 1945 it was announced that the trials of Goering, Ribbentrop and many other German war criminals would begin at Nuremberg in Bavaria on 1st September. The headquarters for the war trials would be set up by Justice Jackson, chief counsel of the United States on the War Crimes Commission, on 15th August and an advance party was already trying to get sleeping accommodation for 8,000 people who were to attend the sessions. Goering and Ribbentrop were to be housed in the local municipal "gaol" during the trials, which were expected to last several weeks. According to a report on the same day from Norway, Quisling was "either made or pretending to be made". Under Norwegian law at the time, "lunatics" could not be punished. Later that month it emerged that the top Nazi war criminals could be tried for crimes they committed prior to the Second World War. It could mean indictment for the disturbances in Czechoslovakia and Poland that preceded the War and included a long list of acts, including deportation to slave labour and devastation "not justified by military necessity". Crimes against peace and crimes against humanity were also listed in the tribunal's jurisdiction. Procedure at the trials was expected to largely follow the lines of British criminal courts, but the joint military tribunal in charge of the trials, which would consist of four members from each country, would not be bound by technical rules of evidence. The Big Powers, who announced their decision about pre-war crimes, also stated that Austria was to be completely separated from Germany. On 13th August 1945 it emerged that Franz von Papen, mystery diplomat and intriguer of two wars, would be one of the first to stand trial at Nuremberg. He was to appear both as a witness against other top Nazis and as a defendant. Ribbentrop was to appear at the same time.

Three days later the papers reported that officials of the United Nations War Crimes Commission spent VJ-Day sending out their 13th list of "minor" war criminals. It was estimated that more than 1,200 European "gangsters" would be sent to jail or the gallows, and that Japanese officials and soldiers guilty of atrocities would be punished in the same way as their German counterparts. The list naming the 1,200 brought the number of "minor" war criminals to an estimated 6,000. Each Japanese prisoner was to be forwarded for justice to the country of his victim. At around the same time, Dr George Mayer, a "butcher of the Jews", told the Allied authorities that Hitler, Himmler, Goebbels, Heydrich and Kaltenbrunner (who succeeded Heydrich as chief of the Security Police) were the men who planned to "exterminate the Jews in Europe". A "conference held in Berlin in 1940 agreed to kill off all Jews. Those unfit for heavy work were to be killed immediately, by gassing if possible. Those fit for work were to be worked until they dropped, and then murdered." Mayer admitted that he was police commissioner in Balbianice, a Polish city in which a ghetto of 8,000 Jewish people was set up. It was known that 4,000 of these people had been gassed, and that the remaining 4,000 had "disappeared". Mayer protested that he was absent in Norway when this happened, and remained arrogant in captivity. He was the first high-ranking Nazi to resist arrest, and had been told that he would probably be sent to Poland for trial by the Russians or the Polish authorities.

Meanwhile, all men aged between 14 and 65 and all women between 16 and 45 in the American zone in Berlin were ordered to register at the local labour bureau. Former Nazis would be given "dirty" jobs to do, while those who lost their jobs under Nazi rule because of their political or religious beliefs were to be given preference. A while later, on 30th August, it emerged that Rudolf Hess was to face trial as a major German war criminal. His name was on the first list of 24 drawn up by the United Nations, and issued in London, Moscow, Washington and Paris. By this time, it was cited that the Nuremberg trials would take place in the late autumn. Julius Streicher, Robert Ley, Alfred Rosenberg and Hans Frank (the governor and "butcher" of Czechoslovakia) were also on the list. Their names were joined by Keitel, Doenitz and Raeder as well as Hjalmar Schacht, von Papen, Von Neubath, Martin Bormann, Gustav Krupp, Ernst Kaltenbrunner, Albert Speer, Wilhelm Frick, Walter Funk, General Jodl, Seyss-Inquart, Baidur von Shirach and Fritz Sauckel.

The trials were postponed on 1st September 1945 when the courthouse floor collapsed, probably due to bomb damage. At this point, Martin Bormann was still on the run, somewhere in Germany it was believed. Meanwhile, Brauchitsch, Commander in Chief of the German Armies, had been found living in isolation on a farm. On 7th September the trial of 48 Polish nationals opened in Paderborn, Germany, where they stood accused of killing seven Germans. The Nuremberg trials, however, looked as though they would be delayed until after Christmas – when Constantin von Neurath would also stand trial, after his capture at Baden-Baden.

On 19th November 1945, writing from Nuremberg, journalist Harry Ashbrook said: "Standing at a point above the stone wall circling the Nuremberg death-gaol I today watched Ribbentrop and Rosenberg and Germany's top war criminals moodily pacing the shell-splintered paths of the prison yard – fit – fully spinning out the last hours before their trial on Tuesday. All were pale, anxious and preoccupied, shuffling round in circles with their hands thrust deep in their pockets. They did not speak to each other as they passed, but some raised their eyes in furtive recognition."

Goering and Hess remained in their second-floor cells. Ribbentrop limped round the yard painfully, according to Ashbrook, with his grey woolen socks bunched under trousers too short for him. "One of the prisoners ran round his path half a dozen times like a professional runner in training; another, his head downcast, angrily kicked at the rubble." Following the suicide of Nazi criminal Robert Ley, prison authorities had worked out elaborate precautions to ensure that no other defendant cheated the Allied tribunal. Special safety lamps were fitted in cells, all hooks and protruding fittings were removed and a guard passed each open grill window every 30 seconds. Even the prisoner barber was only allowed a safety razor, and each blade was checked and double checked. The only item of cutlery prisoners were allowed to use was a spoon. Ashbrook also commented on the eve of the mass trial that Ernst Kaltenbrunner had dropped out of proceedings when he was rushed to hospital suffering from a small haemorrhage at the back of his head.

On 20th November 1945, Rudolf Hess "joked and clowned with Goering, and tried without success to flirt with women court officials", as the US prosecuting counsel, Sydney Alderman, indicted Germany's war criminals. The 20 men in the dock, "looked on unmoved". Hess was described as seeming "like a child". As the prosecuting counsel retold the horrors of the Nazi war, "Hess smiled and ogled spectators in the gallery". It seemed as if he was deliberately attempting to appear unbalanced, with a view to making an insanity plea. The indictment was the most damning and comprehensive document in the history of justice and charged the Nazis in the dock, separately and together, with: "Planning, initiating and waging wars of aggression. Murdering and ill-treating millions of unnamed civilians. Murder on the high seas. Deporting slave labour. Shooting hostages. Plundering and sacking towns and cities."

Major Frank R Wallis, of the US prosecuting staff, quoted speeches by Hitler and extracts from *Mein Kampf* when the trial was resumed on 23rd November. When Major Wallis mentioned the "Master Race" doctrine, Alfred Rosenberg, former Nazi "cultural leader", nodded his head slightly. Major Wallis made his statement after Ralph C Albrecht had opened the prosecution's case on the charge of conspiring to overthrow the Versailles Treaty. He presented a "giant Nazi 'family tree', including the names of several of the accused". The friendships that may have existed between the leading Nazis on trial faded rapidly as the trial progressed. It appeared that each was beginning to realize that all the others were potential witnesses against them. Most sat in the dock chewing gum. Counsel for Rudolf Hess successfully applied for the production of a letter to Hitler left behind before his flight to England. Meanwhile, Eck's execution was postponed and his evidence was taken on commission. The fact that Hess sat reading in court was explained at the end of November when it transpired that he was reconciled to the fact that all those in the dock were to die. "He prefers to amuse himself reading", said his counsel, Dr Rohrscherdt. A medical report had found Hess sane. However, he had twice attempted suicide since his arrest. He also told the court that his "loss of memory" had been fake and that it had been "tactical" to pretend memory loss. He said: "My memory is again in order. The reason I simulated loss of memory was tactical only."

Major-General Erwin Lahausen had escaped being shot in the Hitler bomb-plot purge. As a result, he was able to give evidence at the Nuremberg trials. His evidence clearly shook the men in the dock, and showed that Goering was personally responsible for some of the deeds of Nazi Germany. In his evidence, Lahausen, former deputy chief of Germany's Military Intelligence Service, declared that the Service was led during the war by a man who hated Hitler. One group wanted to kill Hitler, and the other was led by Admiral Wilhelm Canaris, head of the whole intelligence system. As he spoke, for the first time since the trial began, the dock holding the 20 men accused was no longer the centre of interest. All eyes were on the man in the witness box. He told the court that Canaris had warned against the projected shooting and extermination of Polish people. Lahausen said that orders were given to execute British commandos upon their capture, apparently from Hitler. "In our section we all agreed to reject the order because apart from considerations of international law, we should have been responsible for carrying out such measures", he said. Goering's shouts and cries of "traitor", aimed at Lahausen, earned all men in the dock a "telling off" from Colonel B C Andrus of the US army about conduct in court. Goering had lost his "mocking smile" and "flushed with anger, hurled bitter comments across the court" at the witness giving evidence. He had also shouted at General Erich von dem Bach Zelewski, who gave damming testimony, incriminating the whole German High Command for atrocities on the Eastern Front. An ardent Nazi since 1930, Zelewski, who held virtually every German military honour, had been a soldier since he was 15, and told the court that he was making his confession "because I have found my conscience".

In another courtroom in Japan on 25th January 1946, war criminal Captain Kaichi Hirate was sentenced to death. After sentence was passed, the prosecutor read a letter from the mother of Private Raymond Suttle, of Hadleigh, Suffolk, UK, one of the four men of whose death Hirate, a camp commandant, was found guilty. It said: "We are so glad the Americans are trying Hirate, and if you can get into communication with the tribunal I beg you to send them this message... I know you'll do your best for his brokenhearted mother. They have murdered my lovely curly-headed, blue-eyed baby." Mrs Suttle told the *Daily Mirror* that her son was one of the last to be evacuated from Dunkirk and died after being stripped by his Japanese captors and made to spend 10 days and nights in an "icebox room".

Back in Nuremberg, Hermann Goering's first "performances"

in the witness box were of an unrepentant Nazi, glowing with loyalty to Hitler. After his first two and a half hours, Hess greeted him with the words: "You were good." Goering told the court that after he joined the Nazi Party it was agreed that at the start he should remain in the background, but that later he should take over the leadership and from then on make his influence felt. "The Führer depended on me" said Goering with pride, calling himself "Hitler's Right-Hand Man". Swelling out his chest, he went on: "The Führer knew I would use all my powers to spread our ideals. I have done everything within my personal power to strengthen the Nazi movement and increase it, and in all circumstances, I worked to bring it into power."

On 11th May 1946, Karl Doenitz, the former commander in chief of the German Navy, "flushed into a blind rage and shouted his replies" at the trial. "We rescued crews with the greatest devotion", he said. British prosecutor Sir David Makwell Fyfe was not impressed, and kept on with a cross-examination that lasted five and a half hours. Doenitz finally admitted his view was that neutral ships coming into an operational zone could be sunk "any way you wanted". A day later, ex-Gestapo member and war criminal Erik Zacharias broke out of Kempton Park prison near Ashford, Middlesex. He was eventually captured by Frank Williams, a green keeper at Ashford Manor golf course, who brought Zacharias down with a flying tackle at the 13th hole.

In other news, it was expressed by the National Canine Defence League that war criminals should be used instead of animals in the atom bomb experiments to be held in the Pacific. "We'd like to see Nazi and Jap leaders take the place of these innocent animals" said an official.

The court was told that the massacre of 11,000 Polish officer prisoners near Smolensk had been ordered in a secret document. On 28th September 1946, the German news agency (Dana) planned a "tremendous blaze of publicity for the judgment on Goering and 21 other Nazis". A Dana spokesman said: "We are going to make sure this is a day the German people will never forget. We are starting at 9.00 am and from then on we shall be broadcasting every half hour to the German people on a nationwide hook-up – the first since the end of the war, giving them spot reporting and comments until turned nine at night. This will be done by four Germans, one from each zone of Germany – Russian, British, American and French. All the 40 newspapers in the American zone will rush out extra editions all Tuesday afternoon as Justice Lawrence, for the Bench of four Judges, announces the verdicts and sentences." Every security precaution was being tightened, and new passes to the courtroom were issued at the last minute. Photographers were to be barred, while the numbers of military police were increased. "Final decisions, presumably about executions and imprisonments, are being arrived at this afternoon here in the court-house where a Four-Power military mission from the Control Council in Berlin is sitting", wrote the *Daily Mirror*.

On 30th September 1946 it was judgment day, when the 21

deflated Nazis in the dock at Nuremberg, before the world, would hear the summing up of the case. Charged with murder, pillage and torture, the 21 men had spent 10 months on trial. The judges were to begin reciting their findings. Reading the judgment was expected to last the whole day. Verdicts were expected the following day on the six Nazi organizations deemed criminal, along with the verdicts and sentences upon the 21 accused. One at a time, they would stand in the dock to hear their fate. Many of the men, it was known, wanted to be shot should the death penalty be decided. However, Hess, it was cited, expected a "last-minute miracle" to save him.

Each man was expected to clean his own cell before being led into the dock on 1st October 1946. It was to be their last time in front of the judges. The previous day, they had read through their 250-page decision. The prisoners were charged on four main counts, and it was clear none would be cleared on all counts. The evidence of criminality against individual members of the accused was "clear and convincing". They could not shelter under the plea that Hitler ordered them to commit crimes. The war was a deliberate aggression, carried out with systematic, planned terror – and the men deliberately undertook it and were responsible. It was cited that: "They have been responsible in large measure for miseries and suffering that have fallen on millions of men, women and children." The SS and Gestapo were found guilty of being criminal organizations. Goering, who was up first at the tribunal, sat with his head resting on his hand, listening to proceedings

War Crimes

without emotion, as the judges described the horrors of slave labour, organized looting and all the other war crimes of which the men stood accused. The judges ended with: "A thousand years will pass and this guilt will not be erased."

Sentenced to die were Goering, Ribbentrop, Keitel, Kaltenbrunner, Rosenberg, Frank, Frick, Strelcher, Sauckel, Jodl, Seyss-Inquart and Bormann. Those sentenced to life imprisonment included Hess, Funk and Raeder. Speer and von Schirach were given 20-year sentences. Von Neurath received 15 years, while Schacht, von Papen and Fritsche were acquitted.

A total of 12, including the absent Bormann, were sentenced to death by hanging – the most dishonourable fate in the German code. It was known that many would appeal. Keitel wanted to appeal to be shot rather than hanged, Hess wanted his sentence quashed, and it wasn't known on what grounds Goering would appeal. The 316-day trial ended with Justice Lawrence announcing that the Russian judge had dissented and that the judgment had not been unanimous. He had wanted the death sentence for Hess, punishment for those acquitted and condemnation as a criminal conspiracy for the German Cabinet, General Staff (which was found not guilty of being a criminal organization) and the High Command.

The whole scene was fairly unemotional as the sentences were read out. Those acquitted had been fairly confident for some time that they would be. By 11th October, it was known that all appeals for clemency had been rejected by the Allied Control Council. The council also rejected pleas by Goering, Jodl and Keitel to be shot instead of hanged. The news of the rejection of their appeals for clemency was broken to the condemned men on 13th October in the Nuremberg jail. As the guilty men waited in their cells, unaware that they would be executed on 16th October 1946, Field Marshal Kesselring, ex-commander of the German forces in Italy, was flown under armed escort to Germany on his way to Italy to face trial on atrocity charges. The Nazis found guilty at Nuremberg were all executed between 1.00 am and 2.15 am on 16th October. Britain's chief executioner, Albert Pierrepoint, was secretly flown to Nuremberg to supervise the arrangements, while the actual executions were carried out by US army executioners. Goering cheated the hangman by poisoning himself the night before his planned execution.

In June 1961, it emerged that 2,000 boys had desperately struggled to look taller than they really were in 1944. The boys had all been paraded on a football ground at Auschwitz concentration camp, where the "Angel of Death", Josef Mengele – a doctor in the SS – was in charge. It was the eve of the Jewish Day of Atonement, where according to Jewish belief, God passes mankind under his shepherd's rod and decides who shall live and who shall die. Mengele was to choose 1,000 of the younger, thinner boys to be killed in the gas chambers. The way the barbaric doctor made his choices were described on 7th June 1961 by an Auschwitz survivor during the trial of Adolf Eichmann, who was accused of organizing the murder of 6 million European

Jews. Jossef Kleinman, a 31-year-old survivor, told the court in Jerusalem: "Dr Mengele got angry because a boy of 14 or 15 pretended to be 18. He had a plank nailed across a football goal, just above the boy's head. Then he told us all to file under the plank. Those whose heads did not reach it were taken to die.

"They all stretched as high as they could. Everybody wanted to grow another half inch. I despaired. I was only 14. And I saw that taller boys than me were unable to reach the plank." Kleinman said that his 16-year-old brother helped to stuff his shoes with rags and stones to make him taller, and twice the brothers dodged out of the crowd waiting to be tested and into the group that had proved tall enough. The first time Mengele spotted them and ordered them back, but the second time the brothers managed to remain in the tall group. "Half the 2,000 boys failed to pass the test", Kleinman told the court.

Other atrocities by Mengele came to light that same month in the Eichmann trial. Two "gipsy" children were taken to Auschwitz when Mengele wanted more children for his "experiments". The two children were called before the doctor, and when they returned to their living quarters they had been joined together. An Auschwitz survivor, Ver Alexander, told the Israeli court: "The children's veins were stitched together." Judge Moshe Landau presiding asked: "He made them Siamese twins?" Mrs Alexander answered: "He sewed together the children's hands." Another Auschwitz survivor, Raya Kogan, told the court that a woman prisoner named Mallah Zimmerman once escaped the camp with documents recording "special treatment" of "inmates". Special treatment meant killing. Mallah Zimmerman had escaped with a Polish man, but both were caught. The man was tortured and hanged. Before she could be punished, Mallah cut her own wrist with a razor blade and died.

Mengele felt no guilt about killing thousands of concentration-camp victims, stated the *Daily Mirror* in 1985. His 41-year-old son, Rolf, said: "He spoke only of worthless lives. My father was not prepared to repent." Rolf, a lawyer, asked his father – who went on the run – to give himself up. Mengele refused, saying: "For me there are no judges – only avengers." Mengele and his son had last spoken to each other in 1977, when Rolf visited him in Brazil where he was hiding. Mengele probably drowned there in 1979, but efforts remained ongoing in the mid-1980s to positively identify his body. In one letter before he "drowned" Mengele told his son that he was a "gifted man" who could have been a great medical scientist. He added that it was a pity he "should be condemned by fate to live in hiding". Rolf said that his family sent his father money regularly during his 30 years on the run in South America.

While the Nazi atrocities were brought to an end in the mid-1940s, those who survived their heinous crimes lived through the agony for many years afterwards. Families are still affected deeply by the losses, depravation, indignity, starvation and deaths they suffered at the hands of the Nazis. The *Daily Mirror* wrote in October 2012: "They are the images which haunted

Wilhelm Brasse from the moment he pressed the shutter to the day he died." Forced by the Nazis to take photographs of Jewish prisoners, he captured the harrowing stares of frightened children, the emaciated, naked bodies of terror-struck girls, the young victims of grotesque medical experiments and others, all just moments from death. The horrifying pictures from inside Auschwitz, the site of some of humanity's most "evil crimes", were distressing for anyone to look at. "But for the young man who had to take them, each snap brought back unbearable memories which he relived day in, day out, for the rest of his life." The *Daily Mirror*'s journalist M Roper said: "Perhaps no man has ever borne witness to more evil than Wilhelm Brasse, who died this week aged 94." For two years in his early 20s, Wilhelm was the main photographer at the notorious concentration camp where around 1.5 million people met their deaths. A prisoner himself, after refusing to join the German army, he at first believed he was as doomed as the poor subjects who stared down his lens. But he became a "hero" determined one day to tell their stories, and eventually risked his life to preserve thousands of the pictures, despite strict orders to destroy every trace of them. His photos later helped to convict the very Nazi "monsters" who had commissioned them, becoming some of the most damning evidence of their crimes. Wilhelm weighed just six stone when he was freed by US troops at the end of the war. He was too traumatized to ever pick up a camera again. He said in an interview: "Those Jewish kids, and the naked Jewish girls, constantly flashed before my eyes. Even more so because I knew that later, after taking their pictures, they would just go to the gas. I saw all those big eyes, terrified, staring at me. I could not go on. These are things you can never forget."

Born in 1917 to an Austrian father and Polish mother, Wilhelm grew up in the city of Katowice in southern Poland, where he trained as a portrait photographer in a studio owned by his aunt. When Hitler's troops invaded in September 1939, the young man refused to pledge his allegiance to the Reich, despite having to endure several intimidating Gestapo interrogations. A year later, he was captured trying to sneak over the border to Hungary. He was imprisoned for four months, and then given another chance to declare his loyalty to Hitler, but once again he refused. So he was put on a train for the newly opened Auschwitz, a name that would become a byword for systematic mass murder. He once recalled: "The SS chief told us the average life expectancy was two weeks. The strongest would survive for around three months, but it was death in the end, however tough you were. It was constant hitting and kicking and humiliation." Then in February 1941 he was summoned to the office of camp commander Rudolf Hess, who hung himself in prison in 1987 after being found guilty of war crimes. Wilhelm was sure it was his time to die, but instead he was ordered to work as the camp photographer, taking the prisoners' pictures as part of the Nazis' obsession with documenting what they were doing. The job helped save his life, enabling him to get better treatment and food than many others.

For two years he took up to 50,000 photographs of doomed prisoners and witnessed the cruelty these people suffered from SS and Nazi guards. He said: "As the prisoners waited in a queue, the kapos [prisoner overseers] would beat them mercilessly if they made the slightest mistake." One subject was Polish youngster Czeslawa Kwoka, who had a cut lip and bruised face. Wilhelm remembered: "She was so young and terrified. The girl couldn't understand what was being said to her so this woman kapo took a stick and beat her about the face. This German woman was just taking out her anger on the girl. Such a beautiful young girl, so innocent. She cried, but she could do nothing. I felt as if I was being hit myself but I couldn't interfere. It would have been fatal." Czeslawa died at the camp aged 14.

Wilhelm was once asked by the camp doctor to photograph an unusual tattoo of Adam and Eve intricately inked on an inmate's back – then half an hour later he came across the man's dead body, which had been skinned. He said: "The skin with the tattoo was stretched on a table waiting to be framed for this doctor. It was a horrible, horrible sight." Wilhelm was also forced to photograph the victims of Mengele. He said: "Mengele said he wanted me to photograph some of those he was experimenting on. They'd bring the women into the room and strip them naked, then inject them with a kind of anaesthetic – unless they were Jewish, in which case experiments would be performed without anaesthesia." Wilhelm also had to photograph children about to be subjected to appalling acts of sadism, including procedures such as organ removal, amputations and castration, all done without anaesthetic. Then, as the Allies advanced on Berlin in late 1944, the Nazis scrambled to cover up their crimes and ordered all photographs from Auschwitz to be burned. But Wilhelm and another inmate managed to bury tens of thousands of negatives in the grounds of the camp, where they were later recovered. After being freed, he returned home to Poland in July 1945, married and had two children. He tried to work again as a photographer, but was too haunted by his experiences so he opened a business making sausage casings. He carried on being a witness, determined that the stories of the thousands of doomed innocents who, for a brief moment, stood in front of his camera were told. Mengele was fascinated with identical twins and around 3,000 sets of twins were subjected to his barbaric operations. He would "play at 'uncle' Mengele'", offering children sweets and blankets as he trawled the camp for victims. His experiments included sex-change operations and infecting inmates with lethal germs.

It was hoped that the atrocities of the Second World War would never again darken the world, but while Nazi atrocities were brought to an end, there were new crimes and war criminals waiting to perpetrate them into the remainder of the 20th century and beyond.

In 2009, the *Daily Mirror* wrote: "It is a crime so vast that the number of his alleged victims could populate a medium-sized town." Suspected Nazi death camp guard, john Demjanjuk, 89, was finally charged by German prosecutors in July that year with helping to murder 27,900 wartime prisoners. Ukrainian-born Demjanjuk was alleged to have even herded children into the gas chambers at Sobibor in Poland. Munich prosecutors said they had damning wartime documents, including an SS ID card, proving he worked at Sobibor in 1943 and that he was trained at another Nazi facility. American and German experts were said to have declared that the ID document was genuine. Efraim Zuroff, head of Jerusalem's Nazi-hunting Simon Wiesenthal Centre, welcomed the charges and said: "This is a milestone on the way to finally achieving justice. A trial of this sort sends a very important message that even many years after the crimes were committed it is still possible to achieve justice." The retired car factory worker had topped the Centre's list of 10 most-wanted war crime suspects. Each of the 27,900 charges carried a 15-year prison sentence under German law. A court date wasn't set in July 2009, but it would probably be Germany's last major Nazi war crimes case.

Demjanjuk, born in 1920, claimed he was drafted into the Soviet army in 1941, became a German prisoner of war a year later and served at Nazi prison camps until 1944. He denied any role in the Holocaust. His US-based son called the charges "a farce". He insisted: "As long as my father remains alive we will defend his innocence as he has never hurt anyone anywhere." After the Second World War, Demjanjuk emigrated to the US in 1951 and settled in Cleveland, Ohio. Seven years later he became a naturalized American. However, by 1986, he had been stripped of his citizenship and extradited to Israel after he was accused of being "Ivan the Terrible" – a notorious guard at Treblinka concentration camp. He was sentenced to death in 1988, but Israel's Supreme Court overturned his conviction when new evidence showed another man had probably been Ivan. He returned to the US and regained his citizenship, but lost it again in 2002 after the US Justice Department said he had been a Nazi guard at three other camps. In 2005, a US immigration judge ruled he could be deported to Germany, Ukraine or Poland. After a long legal battle, he was sent to Germany in May 2009, where he was taken into custody.

Demjanjuk was found guilty of murdering a total of 28,060 people at his trial in May 2011. More than a dozen family members of his victims were in court in Munich to see the 91-year-old sentenced to five years in prison, but had to suffer the pain of seeing the judge release him pending an appeal six months later. It was the last major Nazi war crimes trial in history. He sat in a wheelchair wearing dark glasses, waiting to hear his fate. There were no living witnesses to place the Nazi collaborator in the Sobibor extermination camp, so prosecutors built their case around the ID card and records that proved he had been a death camp guard. For co-plaintiff Helen Hyde, the headmistress of Watford Grammar School for Girls, the sentence was immaterial. At the time of the trial, it had been 67 years since her aunt, uncle and cousin vanished in the Holocaust. The Neuhaus family, arrested in Holland, arrived at Sobibor on 7th May 1943 and probably died the same day. "He may have dragged them off the train, he may have driven them with his bayonet up to the gas chamber, he may even have pushed them inside", Helen Hyde said. She continued: "It never mattered if he got a day in jail or life; the verdict is what counts, the verdict of history, that the Holocaust happened and that people like him made it happen." Captured as a prisoner of war, Demjanjuk worked for the Nazis in order to save his own life.

Others that evaded the justice of the courts were Milivoj Anner, resident in Austria, whose extradition to Croatia was refused because of dementia, and Alois Brunner, resident in Syria, who was convicted *in absentia* in France. It was believed he could be dead. Algimantas Dailide, resident in Germany, was deported from the US and convicted, but his sentence was never carried out. Klaas Carel Faber, resident in Germany, received life imprisonment, but escaped in 1952. Mikhail Gorshkow, resident in Estonia, was investigated but never charged, while Aribert Heim was thought to have died in Cairo in 1992. Ivan Kalymon, resident in the US, could be extradited, but no country would admit him. Soeren Kam, resident in Germany, was indicted in Denmark, but two extradition requests were refused. Adam Nagorny, resident in Germany, was still under investigation in 2011. However, a Nazi collaborator, suspected of sending thousands to their deaths at the camps in the Holocaust, was charged with war crimes in July 2012. Hungarian Laszlo Csatary, 97, was taken into custody for questioning and put under house arrest at his flat in Budapest. He was a police chief at a holding centre where 12,000 Jewish people were deported to Auschwitz and other camps in 1944. Csatary claimed he was following orders after his country was invaded by the Nazis, but he was accused of the "unlawful torture of human beings", with some reports claiming he regularly used a dog whip on detainees. He was number one on the wanted list of the Simon Wiesenthal Centre. Zuroff said: "When you look at a person like this, you shouldn't see an old frail person, but think of a man who at the height of his physical powers devoted all his energy to murdering or persecuting innocent men, women and children." Csatary was convicted in his absence for war crimes in Czechoslovakia in 1948 and sentenced to death, but he fled to Nova Scotia in Canada the following year and worked as an art dealer in Montreal. He left, bound for Europe, in 1997. The unlawful torture of human beings carried a life sentence, but the charges were dropped in Hungary before he died in August 2013.

The Khmer Rouge

1975–1979

The three most senior surviving members of the Khmer Rouge went on trial for genocide in late November 2011. Pol Pot's right-hand man finally went on trial on 21st November charged with crimes against humanity. Nuon Chea, known as "Brother Number Two", helped orchestrate the genocide that claimed the lives of 1.7 million Cambodians. He was joined on trial by the regime's former head of state Khieu Samphan and foreign minister Ieng Sary. As the tribunal hearing opened, court spokesman Lars Olsen described it as a "major milestone", saying: "Many people never thought it would happen."

Co-prosecutor Chea Leang said the Khmer Rouge "turned Cambodia into a slave camp, reducing an entire nation into prisoners living under a system of brutality that defies belief". The communist regime forced city residents to work in the countryside and purged "enemies of the state". The world was outraged by images of the mass graves known as the "Killing Fields". One third of the entire population was murdered or died of over-work, starvation or torture from 1975 until the regime's fall in 1979. The fight for justice was slow, with the capital Phnom Penh and the UN finally setting up a tribunal in 2006. At this point, only one person had been convicted. Chea, Samphan and Sary, who were all in their 80s, denied the charges against them, including genocide. Pol Pot died in 1998. His brutal regime was behind the deaths of around 1.7 million in the Killing Fields of Cambodia, but as he went on trial for genocide, Khmer Rouge deputy Nuon Chea astonishingly claimed that the murderous thugs headed by Pol Pot were "not bad people". The 85-year-old actually blamed neighbouring Vietnam for the atrocities. He told a court in the capital Phnom Penh: "I don't want the next generation to misunderstand history. I don't want them to believe the Khmer Rouge are bad people, are criminals. It was the Vietnamese who killed Cambodians." Chea saw the regime toppled in 1979 when Vietnam invaded. Former internal security boss Kaing Guek Eav, 69, was convicted in 2010 and sentenced to 35 years in jail.

On 8th May 1975, the incredible story of how the Cambodian capital of Phnom Penh became a "ghost" city after the communist takeover was told by refugees who reached safety. The entire population of 2 million were driven into the countryside at gunpoint by Khmer Rouge troops. They included the sick and the old, and maimed war victims who had to be wheeled and carried out of the capital by their relatives. The story came to light when the last 550 foreign refugees reached the Thai border. According to some eyewitnesses, Cambodians who defied the evacuation order were "shot down like dogs". Phnom Penh was left empty apart from abandoned cooking pots, mattresses, cars and motorcycles together with decomposing bodies littering the streets. A hospital that had 2,000 patients one day was deserted the next. Kand Sith, a Cambodian refugee with a French passport, said: "No one knew where to go when they were ordered to leave. People were screaming. Some pleaded for help. Mothers ran around looking for their children and children searched for their missing parents." British doctor Murray Carmichael said that the communists told the refugees they wanted two months to "clean up the city". After that, the people could return. Other refugees said the townspeople were being set to work in the rice fields. The refugees themselves were among 1,500 people packed inside the French Embassy compound. They faced appalling conditions during the two weeks they waited to be taken to the Thai border. With a shortage of food, they ate once a day, usually rice with tuna fish, peas or canned meat. One desperate group caught and skinned the embassy cat. The communists cut off the water supply, but according to American businessman Douglas Sapper: "They were never harsh to us." The Khmer Rouge troops helped them out with rice, cigarettes, beer and muddy water from the Mekong River. The refugees, however, had heard reports of wholesale executions of Cambodians, but had not witnessed this for themselves. The once peaceful and gentle land of Cambodia in South East Asia, however, had become a human disaster area. More than a third of its 6 million people had been killed by a fanatical regime, whose apparent aim was to wipe out anyone and anything connected with the modern world, and to return the whole nation to "Year Zero", the dawn of an age of slavery, without families and sentiment, without machines, schools, books, medicine or music. The evidence of murder was plentiful – there were cracked skulls, above which were dug mass graves near Angkor Wat by villagers who had lost relatives. For four years, there was almost no contact with the people inside Cambodia; its borders were sealed. John Pilger, for the *Daily Mirror*, sent dramatic reports: "The plane flies low, following the Mekong River west from Vietnam. Once over Cambodia, what we see below us silences everybody on board." There was no one around, no movement, not even an animal. It was as if the great population of Asia had stopped at the border. Whole towns and villages on the river bend stood empty, the doors of houses flapping open, cars on their sides, mangled bicycles in a heap, chairs and beds in the street.

Pilger wrote: "Beside tangled power lines there is the lone shadow of a child, lying or sitting. It does not move. The endless landscape of South East Asia, the patchwork of rice paddies and fields, is barely discernible; nothing appears to grow except the forest and tall, wild grass.

"On the rim of large towns this grass will follow straight lines, as if planned; it is fertilized, we later see, by human compost, by the remains of tens of thousands of men, women and children. All of them murdered."

Cambodia had disappeared from newspaper headlines four years before. Pilger said: "Coming here is like happening on something unimaginable; a human catastrophe and crime without measure. For even Hitler's demonry did not involve the enslavement of the entire population and the systematic slaughter of all those 'touched and corrupted by the twentieth century'... Nor did Stalin's terror include the banning of all learning, all books, all arts, all music and song, and the abolition of the family and all expressions of joy, love and grief, and the destruction of all machines."

All this, and more, did happen in Cambodia, however. Only a few dozen of the former 500-strong royal ballet survived. It had been world-renowned. Of the country's 550 doctors, just 48 remained. The statistics were numbing: 3 million people were "missing", presumed dead. After April 1975, anyone who owned refrigerators, washing machines, hair dryers, generators or typewriters, or who had lived in a city or town, was under virtual sentence of death. Anybody with education or a modern skill was killed if his or her identity was revealed. In fact, doctors, teachers, technicians, skilled workers and even schoolchildren were all at risk. The images were numbing. Pilger wrote: "An emaciated child walks alone down the centre of a main boulevard that once was filled with traffic in a capital city that held 2.5 million people; gangs of children scavenge in the garbage. They are mostly orphans and they are either infants or more than five years old; few of those born during the period of terror appear to have survived." He wrote how young adults were also difficult to find – as if an entire generation had gone. He said: "Indeed, this is now a nation of mostly children, isolated from the world and facing starvation of such intensity that not even a comparison with Biafra is adequate. Who did this? How could it happen?"

In the spring of 1970, Cambodia's tranquillity had been terminated by the greatest saturation bombing in history. This was the secret war launched by President Nixon and Henry Kissinger in violation of American constitutional law and in defiance of Congress. Pilots were sworn to secrecy and their operational logs were falsified or destroyed. For three years, the American public knew nothing about it. By 1973, the equivalent, in tons of bombs, of five Hiroshimas had fallen on neutral Cambodia. The military aim was the destruction of a mythical Vietcong base in Cambodia. President Nixon's aim was to show the Vietnamese communists how "tough" he could be. His policy was the "Madman Theory of War". This threw Cambodia into turmoil; the delicate balance of royalists, republicans and communists of varying shades were destroyed, and Prince Sihanouk, the jazz-loving ruler who had preserved the balance, was overthrown by the military. In the forests, a small group of fanatics, whom the Prince called the Khmer Rouge, and who were inspired by the Red Guards of China's "cultural revolution", intensified their own activities. They declared 1975 "Year Zero", the beginning of the end of the modern world. The ideological aim of their revolution was to recreate a "pure" rural society, "classless and glorious", similar to that of the Khmer empire of the 10th century. Because there were so few of them – they represented probably no more than 10 per cent of the people – this meant controlling the population by enslaving it and reducing it by half. "Their leaders were at first anonymous, deferring constantly to 'The Angkar', or 'the organisation' whose Orwellian 'wisdom' justified everything, including mass blood-letting. But one man, calling himself Pol Pot, emerged at the head."

Little was known about him in 1979, except that he was one of a group of Cambodians who had learned their politics in anarchist circles in Paris in the late 1940s. He claimed to have been a Buddhist priest and a teacher; in fact, he came from a wealthy family and his dreams of a classless society ended with himself. Mao was his hero, and he was to be Cambodia's Mao, an Asian pharaoh. He was, in all probability, a psychopath. At 7.30 am on 17th April 1975, the Khmer Rouge entered the capital city and at 1.00 pm ordered that all residents should leave. There were no exceptions. The hospitals were emptied at gunpoint; doctors were forced to stop mid-operation. Dying patients were wheeled into the streets in their beds. One teacher was not allowed to go home for his family before being ordered to march north; he never saw them again. The little children in his care died of exhaustion or hunger. He only survived by disguising himself as a peasant – the only accepted class – and he changed his personality. When the Vietnamese army drove into Phnom Penh in January 1979, they found the city almost as if it had been abandoned. Their arrival brought four and a half years of terror to an end.

In the city centre there was no electricity. There were no sewerage systems or drinking water – the drains and reservoirs remained polluted with bodies. Even money had no place – it was no longer an acceptable form of exchange, so even new bank notes littered the pavements, and money literally blew about the streets. An elderly woman huddled over a pot of gruel with three children. They were probably the poorest people on earth, but they cooked on a fire fuelled by money. Those few people that were seen looked terrified. Everyone was starving. One man and his remaining son described how he and his family had to work from three in the morning until 11 at night. His wife and three other boys died from overwork and starvation. The man himself was blind. He had always been blind in one eye, but when he cried at the death of his family, the Khmer Rouge took out his other eye with a whip. The horrific stories continued as Pilger made his way through the deserted city. "The barbarism was not always random. It was also highly organized." The chief aim was to reduce the population to less than 2 million – to a single generation untainted by the old life. "If you want to live", the Khmer Rouge cadres told the townspeople, "you must surround your lives with silence. Hear nothing, know nothing, understand nothing." The rules were explicit. People were to live in collective farms, in straw-roofed barracks without walls, so that they could be watched all the time. They would be fed according to how "productive" they were, and this usually meant a tin of rice twice a week. One woman was forced to work in the fields at night, leaving her six-month-old baby alone without a roof, food or care of any kind. The baby was dead within two days. A young student was beaten to death for simply smiling at a young woman. She was about to be thrown down a well, but was saved by the arrival of the Vietnamese. The camp "controller" was the only one who could sanction marriage, and married couples were only permitted to meet once a month. Young boys were recruited as "spies" and listened from the rafters for evidence of laughter or sorrow. Even the word sleep was banned – only the word "rest" was allowed. Examination of the skulls of the dead revealed that a hammer was the most common method of killing. Pilger wrote of a camp that resembled Auschwitz: "It was once a school and was re-named the Tuol Sleng Extermination Centre. Like Auschwitz it has a fence of double barbed wire. Like the victims of Auschwitz, many of the prisoners were brought by train, 150 to a carriage, and the weak seldom survived. It was run by a Gestapo unit called S 21 which was divided into an interrogation unit and a torture and massacre unit. In the former classrooms, where people were mutilated on iron beds, their blood and tufts of their hair are on the floor; so much of it."

Between December 1975 and June 1977, some 12,000 people died slow deaths in the camp – a fact that was easy to confirm because the killers, like the Nazis, were pedantic in their sadism. They photographed people before, and after, they were killed. They recorded their names, ages and even their height and weight, and, like at Auschwitz, there was a room filled to the ceiling with their clothes and shoes, many of them children's. The Vietnamese found eight survivors at the camp, including four children and a one-month-old baby. Eam Chan and Van Nath, a sculptor and painter, survived because they were made to make busts and paintings of Pol Pot. One man who survived, Ing Pench, whose crime was being a teacher, said he lived because he never stopped dreaming. Even when his hand was held in a vice he dreamed of his four sons – even though they were all dead. By this time, Pol Pot was in China where he'd sought refuge, and the Cambodian government was still recognized by the United Nations. Also by this time, Nixon had been disgraced for domestic crookedness, although Kissinger – a Nobel Peace Prize winner – was still deemed a statesman. The legacy of these three men, however, was a famine so severe that in the words of one of the few relief officials "we have just six months to save 3 million people." The United Nations had been formed so that the atrocities of the Second World War could never happen again – but in Cambodia, it had happened again.

The *Daily Mirror* shocked the world when it broke the news about the slaughter of millions of innocent men, women and children in Cambodia by the barbaric Khmer Rouge and their leader Pol Pot. For 10 years between 1979 and 1989 Vietnamese soldiers protected the country, but when they pulled out the world's superpowers were gambling with the nation's fate once again. Peace talks broke down as warring factions jockeyed for position, and Pol Pot and his henchmen appeared to be on the rise once again. They had claimed back some power, the nation was fragile and a Killing Fields genocide was a distinct possibility yet again. A baby girl just a few hours old was pictured in the

War Crimes

Daily Mirror towards the end of September 1989. She had no name, weighed just two pounds and was too weak to feed from her mother. She was born in a dirt-floor hospital in the doom-laden atmosphere of "Site Eight", a Khmer Rouge refugee camp in Thailand. Struggling for survival, she lay in her mother's arms on a crude split-cane bed – a tiny hostage in the continuing battle of Cambodia's Killing Fields.

She was a pawn that had been cynically used to ensure that food kept flowing from the United Nations into the mouths of "an evil army" that should have been brought to justice and disbanded many years before. "Stop the food and we will not allow your doctors to treat our sick" they told the international relief agencies working in the country. Then the baby girl with no name would die. The *Daily Mirror* asked: "what hope is there for her if she lives?" Cambodia had two faces. One was a country of 7 million cheerful, hard-working people who had been cut off from the rest of the world for 10 years as a cynical punishment by the West because they were "freed by the wrong side – Vietnam". The other face was made up of between 500,000 and a million people in refugee camps just over the border in Thailand, who were given food and aid from the West through the United Nations Border Relief Operation. However, because the Khmer Rouge was the most powerful part of a hotch-potch coalition "government in exile" that ruled these people it still occupied the Cambodian seat at the UN. It still received food with "Produce of the USA, not for resale" stamped all over the packages and it still attacked lorry loads of civilians. It continued to maim women, children and farmers with plastic mines planted among the paddy fields, and despite all protests to the contrary, the "civilian" camp where the child with no name was born was really a military base. "Soldiers? There are no soldiers here" said Mey Mann, the Khmer Rouge administrator – but he was lying through his teeth. Out of 30,000 people, 1,500 men had lost one or both legs. The artificial-limb centre was the busiest place around. "Yet they insisted there were no soldiers" wrote the *Daily Mirror*. "These are the people that Mrs Thatcher defended on BBC's *Blue Peter*" the article continued, when she said: "There are reasonable people within the Khmer Rouge." She was asked how she knew that. Her reply: "People who know." Down back streets and on wasteland they played bowls and volleyball and gambled or strolled around with women – soldiers back from the fighting for rest and recreation. The reason for the charade was that no one in Site Eight wanted to rock their "well-fed" boat. Lorries groaning under tons of food trundled in every week. As fast as it arrived, much of the rice vanished, tightly packed into the rucksacks on the soldiers' backs.

For years, the US, China and Russia used Cambodia – sandwiched between Thailand and Vietnam – as a battleground. Then came Pol Pot, the most heinous "monster" since Hitler. He had a mad vision of a peasant culture and started the massacre of doctors, lawyers and teachers. He killed anyone wearing glasses and destroyed the country's money. In three years his murderous army slaughtered at least 1.5 million innocent men, women and children. Eventually he was driven out by Vietnamese troops, but their peace-keeping forces couldn't afford to stay any longer. In 1989, both the US and China were pushing for the Khmer Rouge killers to rule Cambodia once again.

Well-trodden gaps in the perimeter fence at Site Eight led towards the Khmer Rouge's Voz military bases nearby. The closed bases were even worse than the refugee camps. A horrified doctor told how he was herded out of a hospital ward in Voz Four when the administrator charged through a ward pulling out all the intravenous tubes from malaria patients. He had decided that quinine was the wrong treatment. In was in an attempt to paint a more acceptable image of themselves that the Khmer Rouge opened Site Eight to Western journalists as a showpiece camp. They boasted that they even had a Buddhist temple, but the building was on the far edge of the camp and on land pockmarked by shell-holes. It stood right where the shelling had fallen when the Khmer Rouge started moving the women and children up towards the Cambodian border. In reality, this was the future for the baby girl with no name who lay struggling for life in the hospital.

A 12-year-old boy, so small and frail that he looked half that age, lay unconscious and semi-naked in the heat while two medical assistants worked urgently around him. San Lok was brought to a hospital in Takeo, a gutted, shattered town reeling from war. His mother sat on the edge of his cot, holding one small hand, gently stroking his arm. Tears were streaming down her face. One nurse gave him a heart massage, squeezing his bird-like chest. Another worked at a small portable respirator, which all but covered the child's face. She pumped at the black rubber bellows, trying to breathe some air into reluctant lungs. San Lok had measles – a simple childhood disease – but in a land short of hospitals and roads, and no hope of a telephone, it took a long time to get him to doctors when complications set in. There were few drugs and no modern machines, so the nurses tried to revive the small boy as best they could. Within a few minutes the child died. With grief etched across her face, San Lok's mother's tears dropped onto the still body. She pulled his meagre clothing over his body to give him some dignity in death.

At another hospital 40 miles away, the Australian Red Cross were struggling to patch up the ravages of war. The Khmer Rouge had ambushed a crowded lorry near Kampon Speu, in southwest Cambodia not far from their bases on the Thai border. One doctor was still shaking two days later, shocked, unable to believe the horror he had seen. "The Khmer Rouge blew up the lorry with rockets" he said. "The first rocket hit the fuel tank and it went up like a torch. Burning fuel exploded everywhere, setting people on fire. Then the Khmer Rouge came out of the jungle and sprayed the burning bodies with machine gun fire." There were up to 100 people on the lorry – no one knew exactly how many. In this part of the world they acted as buses. Passengers piled on until there was no more room, along with their bicycles,

War Crimes

chickens and pigs, and then even more piled on top. When the attack was over, another lorry came across the scene. The passengers piled the dead and dying into it and rushed them to a provincial hospital. At least 50 were dead, as they counted the bodies in the dirt outside the hospital. Inside, with primitive equipment, the Australians did their best for the men, women and children now in their care. They had suffered massive burns and bullet wounds. Nothing had changed. The Khmer Rouge had no intention of changing their ways. They forced girls as young as 15 to carry food and ammunition through thick jungle and over the mountains into Cambodia from the border camps in Thailand. The human slave chain was vital to the guerrilla effort as the murdering and maiming continued unchallenged. One of their load carriers, 23-year-old Sok Sam Bo, managed to escape. She told of her long ordeal with the Khmer Rouge. The human chain totalled 1,000 women in single file, walking 15 feet apart so that if one stepped on a landmine only a couple of others would be blown up as well. Sok Sam Bo said: "Yes, we were very frightened. But, we were more frightened not to go. If we refused, they stopped giving us food until we did, or wouldn't let us have hospital treatment."

They carried sacks strapped to their shoulders, each bag weighing around eight stone. In the bottom of the sacks was rice, which was weighed down by clean clothes. An artillery shell, a rocket or ammunition pouch containing machine-gun bullets was tied on either side. Each woman also carried another shell on one shoulder. They walked by day for seven days into the Killing Fields to deliver their deadly cargo. Travelling light, the return journey took three days. Sok Sam Bo started at the age of nine. At 17 she was married to a Khmer Rouge platoon commander and at the age of 19 gave birth to his son. A little later, her husband was killed in battle – she wasn't informed for 10 months. Finally, in 1989, Sok Sam Bo and her sister Sok Ta, 18, bribed their camp guards and paid Thai guides to take them from the Khmer Rouge camp to Site Two, one of the better official refugee camps.

Almost a year later, the US launched a dramatic bid to stop a new "Killing Fields" slaughter in Cambodia. Pol Pot's power was gaining momentum, but in a "sudden about face" the US decided to back Vietnam and China to halt another Khmer Rouge bloodbath. Two years later, in December 1992, three British servicemen were held hostage in the Killing Fields. They were among six members of a UN peace-keeping patrol kidnapped by Khmer Rouge guerrillas who accused them of being spies. Fears for the men's safety grew when a UN helicopter sent to look for them was blasted with gunfire by the guerrillas. A French officer on board was seriously wounded before the bullet-scarred chopper managed to limp back to the capital. The Britons included Royal Navy Lieutenant Scott Verney, Welsh Guards Captain Richard Williams and Royal Artillery Lieutenant-Colonel Mark Walton. They were unarmed on a jungle river when they were ambushed at gunpoint, along with a New Zealander and two Filipino officers. They were freed a few days later.

In March 1993 the Khmer Rouge massacred 36 Vietnamese people. More than four years later, in October 1997, Pol Pot claimed he was framed for the 2 million who died under his Killing Fields regime. The 72-year-old said the mass murders really happened when "the old enemy" Vietnam invaded to topple his Khmer Rouge government in 1979. He insisted: "My conscience is clear. To say millions died is too much." He added: "I want you to know everything I did, I did for my country." When asked if he wanted to apologize for the horror, he looked confused, before replying: "No!" The ex-dictator's defiance came in an interview with a US journalist, the first since his Maoist regime had been ousted. He had led a guerrilla war, but was arrested by his own comrades in a power struggle in 1997 and sentenced at a "show trial" to life imprisonment. Held in a jungle hut with his second wife and 12-year-old daughter, he was unrepentant about seizing power in 1975 and turning his country into a vast labour camp where people were executed, starved and tortured to death. He admitted "mistakes" but blamed Vietnam for planting the mountains of skeletons preserved as monuments to his brutal rule. Having suffered a stroke, he even pleaded for the world to feel sympathy for him. He said: "You don't know what I have suffered." The interview provoked anger among survivors of his genocide when it was shown on TV. One woman said: "I want to kill him. I lost my father when I was just seven years old." Another said that two of her brothers were killed and her father died of starvation. Of the 20,000 people sent to one torture camp in a former school, just seven survived.

On 27th May 1999, two years after the controversial interview, and a year after his death, a newspaper article said that Pol Pot had been executed and did not die of natural causes. The claim came from his former military commander who said that the mass murderer did not die of heart failure. However, Pol Pot was cremated without an autopsy. Ta Mok, who replaced Pol Pot in a power struggle in 1997, alleged he knew who ordered the former leader's execution. At the time Ta Mok – dubbed "The Butcher" – was in jail facing charges of genocide and crimes against humanity.

The *Daily Mirror* reported: "Her hands shake as she reaches up to the rafters of her one-room hut to pull down a photo in a gilt frame that sparkles incongruously through the gloomy poverty." The woman dusted the photo down and gazed at the white-haired old man in the picture. Ho Khoem hesitated before she handed it to the *Daily Mirror* reporter. "That's him" she said through the interpreter, who shuddered at the sight of the memory of the benevolent-looking geriatric. Ho then brought down a second picture, of the same man, in his demonic prime. In this second photograph, a stern black-and-white portrait, he looked far more the career killer. Dressed in a black uniform, his cold eyes stared defiantly, his shoulders "taut with power" and his wife submissive by his side. The man in the photograph is Ta Mok. "Yes, my father did bad things" Ho whispered tearfully, as her teenage daughter skulked in the shadows, listening to her mother speak of the family's "guilty secret" for the first time. At this time it was March 2007 and Ho was unable to totally believe that her father was evil. She confirmed that he wasn't like that at home. Strict, yes, but not evil. She could not quite believe that her father had killed and overseen the killing of babies swung against blades wedged in tree trunks in order to save bullets. It was believed that Ta Mok was personally responsible for the deaths of thousands of people, if not tens of thousands, including a single slaughter in Angkor Chey district in which 30,000 people died. Ho had wanted to ask her father what he had done, but she never dared. While her brothers were given commanding positions in the army, she was sent to take charge of a hospital. She didn't know what was going on until she read about it in the papers. "When the Vietnamese took over in 1979, I had to read about the torture and the slaughters in the newspapers like everybody else. I was in shock. It was the first time I had ever heard what my father had done. The nightmares started, seeing him do those terrible things. I still have nightmares and I still live in fear that one day someone will come to my house and take revenge on me and my daughter as we sleep. I do not sleep very much."

Ta Mok was one of the few former Khmer Rouge leaders to be charged with genocide, before others were brought to trial in 2011. Ta Mok had been going to stand trial in front of a panel of Cambodian and international US-selected judges in 2007, but he died in jail at the age of 81 the year before. At this point, only one of his former comrades remained in custody, Kak Kek leu, known as "Duch". He oversaw the slaughter of 10,499 "spies and traitors" and 2,000 children at the capital's Tuol Sleng Extermination Centre. Some of the more minor members of the regime still enjoyed privileged positions in the army and government – including Prime Minister Hun Sen, who wasn't implicated in any war crimes. Ho had only seen her father twice in the seven years he was in jail before his death. He was angry that at the time he was the only leader being prosecuted. She revealed that he had also threatened to expose an alleged American and British role in equipping Khmer Rouge guerrillas, long after the world knew of the genocide, to fight their communist enemies in Vietnam. Despite his terrible legacy, little was known of the man who they called "The Butcher". He was born to an affluent farming family and spent time studying to become a Buddhist monk. However, he abandoned his studies and his family in order to join the revolutionaries. Ho said that no one knew why he went from being a good monk to a slaughtering fighter. Her own husband was killed by a mine, and she was earning less than a dollar a day selling rice wine and tins of food from her shack in a village 40 miles from the former Khmer Rouge stronghold of Battambang. It was a hard life for her and the other villagers, all former Khmer Rouge cadres and their families, cut adrift by history and still reviled by the nation. Yet, Ho had everything she ever wanted as a child, living in comfortable surroundings in a big house, never knowing why her father wasn't at home much and the atrocities he was committing. Of the 175 villagers she now

War Crimes

lived amongst, some were responsible for atrocities, including one woman who ran a beer stall who had previously worked in a concentration camp. Others were simply foot soldiers, indoctrinated as children. For them, the future was bleak, no matter what happened at the tribunal in Phnom Penh. Ho said: "I worry about our children. They are being punished for the sins of their parents. My daughter has no chance of ever getting out of here – no education, no job. We have been left here to rot."

The chief torturer of the Khmer Rouge, Duch, wept on 27th February 2008 as he showed the judges at his trial the mass graves of his victims in the Killing Fields. He was charged with crimes against humanity after his arrest for the massacres and his role as commandant of the notorious s-21 prison. He led 80 judges and lawyers around former rice fields outside the capital where 129 graves were uncovered after the Vietnamese invasion. A policeman said: "I saw Duch kneel in front of trees where Khmer Rouge soldiers smashed children to death. He cried and apologised to the victims." About 14,000 people were sent to jail to be tortured into confessing to working against the communist regime. Few emerged alive. Duch was expected to be a key witness in the trials of Brother Number Two, Nuon Chea. Duch claimed that he was merely following "orders from the top". However, survivor Chum Manh, 78, said: "I want to hear him explain why he jailed me and killed my wife and our baby."

Ieng Thirith, 76, appeared in court in May 2008. She was Pol Pot's sister-in-law and Cambodia's social welfare minister, and prosecutors said she must have known of tens of thousands being killed. She denied the charges of "crimes against humanity". Three years later, Nuon Chea, faced the genocide tribunal. He was also charged with crimes against humanity.

War Crimes

Iraq and Saddam Hussein

1979–2003

One of the most notorious dictators of the 20th century, Saddam Hussein's reign as the fifth president of Iraq ran from his rise to power in 1979 until he was deposed by a coalition of US and UK forces in 2003. In the intervening 24 years, Hussein was responsible for suppressing several uprisings (both Shi'a and Kurdish) and the brutality of his dictatorship was widely condemned.

A video of his interrogation was released prior to his trial for 14 war crimes, which showed the Iraqi tyrant relaxed and stroking his beard. He was quizzed in particular over a relatively unknown massacre in 1982 at Dujail, 50 miles north of Baghdad.

Around 100 died in the Shi'a village of Dujail, it was claimed, in revenge for a roadside ambush on Saddam's motorcade as it passed through the area. A total of 18 would-be assassins were believed to have perished in a gun battle with his secret police. Hours later, a special forces unit rampaged through the village, allegedly killing dozens more people and destroying Dujail's date groves.

The scale of the slaughter did not compare with the other charges filed against him though. Up to 5,000 died in an infamous chemical-weapons attack on the Kurdish town of

Halabja in 1988, while another of the 14 accusations related to the execution of 8,000 members of the Barzani tribe – a powerful Kurdish clan.

But Dujail was significant because prosecutors were hoping to find evidence of Saddam's direct involvement. Sources said that his half-brother Barzan Ibrahim al-Tikriti and former Vice-President Taha Tassin Ramadam would testify that he personally ordered the killings.

It was thought that this could become a successful "test case", avoiding lengthy hearings about other war crime claims, denying Saddam a political platform and ending in a death sentence. The recording of the pre-trial investigations was made public by the Iraqi special tribunal that would eventually try the dictator, who was being held in prison in Baghdad.

Saddam had heavy bags under his eyes, his hair was unkempt and his beard was more flecked with grey than before. The video had no sound, but observers were able to lip-read comments by presiding judge Raad Jouhi, who told Saddam at one point: "Answer the question, answer the question!"

It was said that Saddam's morale had collapsed because of the charges he faced. Many of the 14 offences to be put to him carried the death penalty. In addition to the Dujail, Halabja and Barzani incidents, they included the 1987–88 Anfal campaign – a depopulation plan in which hundreds of thousands of Kurds were killed or expelled from northern Iraq.

The forced emigration of thousands of Shi'a Fayli Kurds into

Iran was another allegation, while Saddam's 1990 invasion of Kuwait, which led to the first Gulf War, was a further indictment. He was also accused of draining southern marshes following the 1991 Shi'a uprising, turning an area rich in fish into an arid salt bed.

The trial lasted until November 2006, and when the verdict came Saddam Hussein reacted as he had throughout his year-long trial – with arrogance, defiance and utter contempt. First, he refused to stand up before Judge Rauf Abdel Rahman, and had to be hauled to his feet by two court bailiffs. Then, as the death sentence was announced, the 69-year-old fallen tyrant tried to drown out the judge's words, yelling: "God is Great. You are servants of the occupiers. You are traitors." But he could not stop Judge Rahman's voice from ringing out around the Baghdad court: "Death by hanging. Death for committing crimes against humanity." As the judge told the bailiffs "Take him out", Saddam's face contorted with fury. He clenched his hands and shouted: "Life for the glorious nation and death to its enemies. To hell with the enemies of Iraq. To hell with the occupiers. To hell with the betrayers." Throughout the sentencing Saddam appeared visibly shaken. But, as he was led from the building, he recovered his composure and even managed to smile. Saddam was sentenced to death for ordering the massacre of 148 people in the Shi'a village of Dujail in 1982, although his lawyers were launching an immediate appeal. President Bush welcomed the verdict, calling it "a milestone in the Iraqi people's efforts to replace the rule of a tyrant with the rule of law. It's a major achievement for Iraq's young democracy and its constitutional government."

Soon after the verdict there were reports of violence in many areas of Iraq. Within minutes, police in Baghdad were reporting one woman had been killed and 10 people wounded by celebratory gunfire as citizens poured onto the streets in defiance of an all-day curfew. State television broadcast images of delighted Iraqis, superimposed on footage of mass graves and killings from the Saddam era.

The scenes of joyful, chanting crowds were repeated in Shi'a-dominated areas of the country, but in Sunni-dominated areas, the stronghold of Saddam's Baath Party, the mood was very different. In Tikrit, Saddam's home town, a 1,000-strong crowd carried pictures of the dictator and shouted: "We will revenge you."

Saddam's execution was carried out on 30th December 2006 at the joint-Iraqi–American military base of Camp Justice near Baghdad.

Saddam's cousin was also sentenced to be hanged in June 2007 for his part in the slaughter of thousands of Kurds. A court in Baghdad passed the death sentence on Ali-Hassan al-Majid – nicknamed "Chemical Ali" – and two other regime officials for masterminding a genocide campaign that killed 180,000 Kurds in northern Iraq. Kurdish towns and villages were targeted by Iraqi jets armed with mustard gas and chemical weapons – a tactic that earned Ali his gruesome nickname. Ali shook in the dock as sentence was passed, then as he was led from the court said: "Thanks be to God." Kurds welcomed the sentence, even though Ali had not been charged with the most notorious attack, a 1988 air raid on the city of Halabja that killed 5,000 people.

Other members of Saddam's regime were found guilty of war crimes in Iraq, but Donald Payne, a corporal in the British army, gained unwanted notoriety in September 2006 when he became the first British soldier to admit to a war crime. Payne, 35, pleaded guilty at a court martial to treating Iraqi civilians inhumanely but denied killing hotel worker Baha Musa, 26.

Seven soldiers were on trial over the death of Mr Musa in Basra in September 2003. Tests found 93 injuries on his body, the court martial at Bulford Camp in Wiltshire was told. It was alleged that another of those detained with Mr Musa suffered kidney failure as a result of the abuse he received. The court heard how Iraqi civilians arrested at a hotel in Basra were held for 36 hours in a disused building. When the civilians were arrested in a swoop at the hotel in 2003, it was believed that they were dangerous insurgents.

Julian Bevan, QC, prosecuting, told Judge Stuart McKinnon that, with temperatures nearing 60 degrees celcius, the prisoners were hooded, deprived of sleep and told to stand in a knees-bent position. They were beaten if they failed. In some cases, they were urinated on and deprived of food and water.

"We are dealing with systematic abuse against prisoners" claimed Mr Bevan, "involving unacceptable violence against persons who were detained in custody, hooded and cuffed and unable to protect themselves".

Payne was alleged to have urged others to lie, and to say that Mr Musa died after falling and hitting his head. Despite Payne's guilty plea to inhumane treatment, "his behaviour went some way beyond what he admits", said Mr Bevan. He added that there was a failure of more senior officers in their duty to protect their prisoners.

Lance-Corporal Wayne Crowcroft, 22, denied a charge of inhumane treatment, as did Private Darren Fallon. Sergeant Kevin Stacey, 29, denied assault and an alternative charge of common assault, while Colonel Jorge Mendonca, 42, denied neglecting his duty along with two other senior officers from the Intelligence Corps – Warrant Officer Mark Davies, 37, and Major Michael Peebles, 35.

Payne routinely kicked, punched and abused the hooded and handcuffed civilians and described their moans and groans as music, it was alleged, with Mr Bevan claiming that Payne asked a fellow soldier: "Do you want to see the choir?" Mr Bevan then alleged that Payne proceeded to "orchestrate" the "choir" and kick each of them in the lower back where the kidneys are located, wherupon at each blow the prisoner cried out in pain.

On the second day of the court martial the court was shown a minute-long video of Payne allegedly mistreating captured Iraqis in detention. Mr Bevan said it was shot by a fellow soldier and later handed over to the authorities after Mr Musa died.

First World War
After his capture by the British, this man was tried for the
crime of spying in August 1915. He was found guilty and
sentenced to execution by firing squad. Both sides used
spies during the First World War. To their own side they
were heroes, yet to their enemies they were cowardly and
treacherous. Fear of spies prompted hundreds of arrests and
a number of executions, many of which might have been of
innocent men and women.

General von Trotha was responsible for the execution of the infamous Hun policy in South-West Africa, which involved the massacre of thousands of native Herero men, women and children. "Kill every one of them" he said, "and take no prisoners". (Hendrik Withier, leader of the Hereros, is pictured inset.)

This group of former British soldiers marches into the Courts of Justice at Leipzig to give evidence at the war crime trials of German personnel in May 1921.

Second World War
Under the dictatorship of Adolf Hitler, Germany committed
atrocities during the Second World War the likes of which the
world had never before seen.

CRISIS MAPS

Sunday Mail

Scotland's National Sunday Newspaper

Red Tape The Whisky

No. 1613   28 Pages   B   SUNDAY, SEPTEMBER 3, 1939   TWOPENCE

MIDNIGHT CABINET MEETING

AT 11.10 last night it was announced that the Cabinet had been summoned again. Within five minutes Ministers were trudging through blackened streets of Westminster in what appeared to be a violent electric storm.

Every second the sky was lit up with violent flashes of blue light. Emergency fire and A.R.P. patrols were called to their stations. The meeting ended at 12.10. No statement to be issued until to-day.

No hint was given as to the purpose of the discussions, though it was believed that it was some further communication from France after last night's House of Commons debate which necessitated the calling together of the Cabinet.

WE DON'T MAKE WAR AGAINST CIVILIANS

"THE GOVERNMENTS OF THE UNITED KINGDOM AND FRANCE SOLEMNLY AND PUBLICLY AFFIRM THEIR INTENTION, SHOULD A WAR BE FORCED UPON THEM, TO CONDUCT HOSTILITIES WITH A FIRM DESIRE TO SPARE THE CIVILIAN POPULATION AND TO PRESERVE IN EVERY WAY POSSIBLE THOSE MONUMENTS OF HUMAN ACHIEVEMENT WHICH ARE

TREASURED IN ALL CIVILISED COUNTRIES.

"IN THIS SPIRIT THEY HAVE WELCOMED WITH DEEP SATISFACTION PRESIDENT ROOSEVELT'S APPEAL ON THE SUBJECT OF BOMBING FROM THE AIR. FULLY SYMPATHISING WITH THE HUMANITARIAN SENTIMENTS BY WHICH THAT APPEAL WAS INSPIRED, THEY HAVE REPLIED TO IT IN SIMILAR TERMS.

Lebrun's Stirring Message

NO REPLY FROM HITLER

ANGLO-FRENCH DECLARATION

Germans Claim Corridor Victory

Germans Repulsed

LATER NEWS

The front page of 4th September 1939's *Daily Record* published accusations that German forces had been using mustard gas in attacks against civilians.

DEWAR'S White Label

Daily Record

NEWSPAPER

MONDAY, SEPTEMBER 4, 1939

GERMAN 'PLANES USE GAS ON CIVILIANS

Churchill Takes Up His Old Post in Cabinet

"I'LL BLOW UP THIS RING" —Hitler

THE POLISH FOREIGN OFFICE ANNOUNCED LAST NIGHT THAT GERMAN 'PLANES ARE DROPPING MUSTARD GAS ON CIVILIAN POPULATIONS. THE ANNOUNCEMENT ALSO ALLEGED THAT GERMAN 'PLANES WERE BRUTALLY BOMBING AND MACHINE-GUNNING CROWDS OF FLEEING AND TERRIFIED WOMEN AND CHILDREN.

FIFTEEN HUNDRED MEN, WOMEN AND CHILDREN WERE KILLED IN AIR RAIDS ON THE POLISH CIVILIAN POPULATION ON SATURDAY ALONE.

WARSAW WAS RAIDED YESTERDAY. THERE IS SCARCELY A TOWNSHIP IN POLAND WHICH HAS NOT SUFFERED FROM AIR ATTACK, ACCORDING TO THE POLISH AMBASSADOR IN LONDON.

9 WILL LEAD IN WAR

POLISH LOURDES BURNING

No Information On Bremen Report

BANKS CLOSED TO-DAY

PREMIER WITH KING AGAIN

FRANCE CALM AT ZERO HOUR

In sharp contrast to the Nazi ideology, the front page of the Scottish *Sunday Mail* of 3rd September 1939 clearly stated that the United Kingdom and France would not wage war against civilians.

Stalin says—Our task is to

EXTERMINATE THESE MURDERERS

FOOLED JAP WARSHIPS, HIT CONVOY

e legless

This is the story

ROMMEL GOT VICHY PETROL

Women stop "all men" inquiry

Homeless by burst balloon

Laundries may take coupons

DEAD NURSE IN PARK — MAN CHARGED

Five German soldiers test the strength of ropes prior to the hanging of five Russian civilians in Smolensk. A German stands by with rifle ready in case any attempt to escape was made. Stalin was quoted as saying: "Hitler wants a war of extermination – he shall have it. From now on our task is to destroy, to exterminate these murderers."

This emaciated prisoner shows the suffering endured in Nazi concentration camps.

This horrific scene shows one of the many mass graves at Belsen concentration camp.

Belsen concentration camp burns, having been set on fire with the use of flamethrowers in May 1945.

A view of the court dock at the Belsen trial. Belsen was one of the more horrific of Hitler's extermination camps. It was officially used as a holding centre from April 1943 until April 1945 when it was liberated, although by that time many prisoners had been gassed or shot.

Nazi officials were made to bury more than 240 of their victims in a wood following the Luneburg War Crimes trial in 1945.

Auschwitz survivors return for a remembrance ceremony at the infamous "execution wall".

The French village of Oradour sur Glane in June 1980. It was here that Nazis virtually wiped out an entire community during the Second World War. The village remains unchanged since that day, with damaged buildings and the wreck of a car from which the mayor was dragged as a reminder and memorial of the past.

Simon Wiesenthal was a survivor of five Nazi death camps during the Second World War, and was credited with helping to bring more than 1,100 Nazi war criminals to justice.

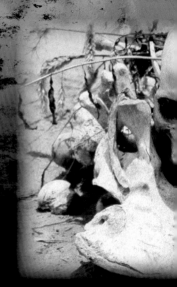

r Rouge

taken from shallow graves near
Wat, Cambodia, in January
fter the Vietnamese army rolled
nom Penh after overcoming
ops of the Khmer Rouge
. The Vietnamese occupation
rned up some disturbing
ce of the murderous policies of
, and was soon finding piles of
remains all over Cambodia.

**12,000 died here. The killers,
like the Nazis, photographed their
victims before and after death**

ECHO

MURDER, NAZI STYLE: clothes and pictures of the victims at the Khmer Rouge's Tuol Sleng "extermination centre." Twelve thousand died here.

OF AUSCHWITZ

VICTIMS: im

...ches, the skulls and bones of some of the thousands murdered by the Khmer Rouge.

Like the Nazis 30 years earlier, the Khmer Rouge photographed their victims before and after their deaths. Around 12,000 Cambodians died in the Tuol Sleng extermination centre.

The bones and skulls of thousands of victims lying in open trenches, September 1979.

Iraq/Saddam Hussein
Royal Scots Dragoon Guards pull down the portrait of former dictator Saddam Hussein after Basra town centre is liberated by British army soldiers in 2003.

Sri Lanka
A sit-down protest in Westminster Square against the treatment of the Tamil people by the Sri Lankan authorities brought traffic to a standstill around central London.

Sierra Leone
Some of the child soldiers, with Felix Musa at the forefront, drawn into the fighting in Sierra Leone in 1999.

A child soldier of the Kamajor Fighters is seen holding a hand grenade as Sierra Leone is gripped in another round of civil war.

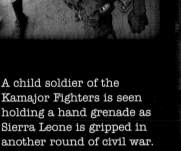

Victims of the civil war: seven-year-old Dambea Camara with her mother, Fina, who had to hold her daughter's hand as it was hacked off.

THE END

Joy of war-torn Liberians as Taylor keeps his promise to quit as leader

Charles Taylor steps down as President of Liberia. He would later be tried for war crimes, convicted and sentenced to 50 years' imprisonment.

Bosnia/Kosovo

A Muslim woman uses a hose pipe to try and dampen down her house, which has been burnt out by Croat forces during the ethnic cleansing in Bosnia in 1993.

A child cries out for water while on a refugee bus in Kosovo in 1999.

A map shows the location of known mass graves in Kosovo in June 1999.

GANG OF EVIL
Bosnia war criminals heading for prison in Britain

CUSTODY: Doncaster prison

EXCLUSIVE
By JEREMY ARMSTRONG

THESE are the nine Bosnia war criminals likely to be locked up in a British jail.

Between them, they are responsible for some of the worst killings in Europe since the Second World War.

They are considered to be so dangerous they will need the supervision by specially trained staff, backed up by round the clock guards.

None will benefit from early release on parole. Some will die behind bars.

All the men will be held in a specially built 11-bedroom unit at high-security Doncaster jail — dubbed "Devastated" by inmates — at a cost of £60,000 a year.

They could ultimately be joined by former Yugoslav president Slobodan Milosevic, Bosnia Serb leader Radovan Karadzic and Radko Mladic, commander of the Bosnian Serb Army, who are all wanted by war crimes.

But Doncaster jail has been beset by security problems and suicides since it opened in 1994.

It last month the worst prison riots in years. The inmate ringleaders are likely to be mixed in with the men, provoking fears the men, after imprisoned, could be at threat from fellow prisoners.

Tihomir Blaskic 45 years for the death of violence in Lasva that left hundreds dead and thousands on the run.

Goran Jelisic Boasted of murdering up to 30 Muslims before breakfast every day. Sentenced to 40 years.

Vlatko Kupreskic Six years for setup and clerical persecution in the horrific massacre in the Lasva river valley.

HELD: Men at a camp in Bosnia during the conflict

Drago Josipovic Found guilty of murder and persecution in the Lasva massacre, and sentenced to 18 years.

Vladimir Santic 25 years for persecution and murder. Must serve two-thirds before being considered for parole.

Mirjan Kupreskic Re-sentenced on appeal to heightened future in which two children died. Sentenced to 8 years.

Zoran Kupreskic 10 years for persecution after court heard of crime carried out with his brother at Lasva.

Haxim Delic Held in Bosnia in 1996, convicted of crimes against humanity and sentenced to 20 years.

Esad Landzo Guilty along with Delic of horrific treatment of inmates at Celebici camp. Given 15 years.

VOICE OF THE MIRROR: PAGE 6

Nine of the men convicted of war crimes in Bosnia.

An ethnically cleansed area in the Bosnian city of Prijedor, where Muslim families were burnt out of their houses by the Serbians.

A boy plays in the streets of Sarajevo, Bosnia, as life in the war-torn city returns to normal.

Picture the world cannot ignore

CARNAGE IN A CHURCH: The bodies of some of the 1,130 victims after the massacre

Rampaging troops killed them with rifles, grenades and spears

Rwanda
Some of the victims massacred in a church in Rwanda in April 1994.

Just a handful of the child orphans in Rwanda following the civil war.

SYRIA MASSACRE HORROR

▼ **INNOCENT** Child victims lie packed in ice yesterday.

NOW THEY'RE GASSING CHILDREN

By CHRIS HUGHES, Security Correspondent

NINE innocent children lie dead in a picture that will horrify the world.

Syrian rebels claim the youngsters were among 1,300 civilians gassed yesterday in a chemical weapons attack by President Assad's embattled regime as part of the nation's brutal civil war.

UN inspectors were urged to investigate last night as Syrian government officials denied the atrocity – described as "a crime against humanity".

FULL STORY: PAGES 4&5

DENIAL Assad

AIR RAID Syrian jets fire missiles at a rebel area yesterday

Chemical weapons kill 1,300, say rebels

Syria

The front page of the *Daily Mirror* for 22nd August 2013 shows some of the children who were victims of a chemical weapons attack in Syria.

Libya
Colonel Muammar
Gaddafi ruled Libya
with an iron fist
following his 1969
coup d'état. His
tyrannical regime
was overthrown
following civil war,
and he was killed in
October 2011.

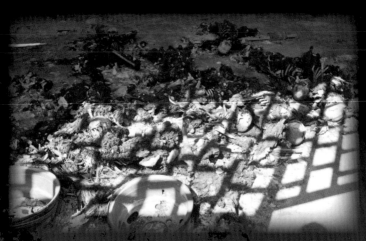

The mass grave of more than 150 freedom fighters who were
sprayed with bullets and hand grenades before being burnt to
death by Colonel Gaddafi's Libyan forces.

The video, taken during 36 hours of alleged continuous torture, showed Payne screaming abuse at the Iraqis. He then forced them into the stress position, where they had to stand parallel to a wall with knees bent and hands outstretched. Mr Bevan told the seven-member panel that Payne "must have known he was being filmed and this only serves to add to the openness in which he treated these men."

At the end of the hearing Colonel Mendonca praised the heroic job his troops did in Iraq – minutes after he and his men were cleared of war crimes – but in November 2009 Payne was quoted as saying that they all kicked, punched and threatened to kill prisoners.

Payne, who became the first British serviceman to be convicted of a war crime when he was jailed for a year, accused commanding officer Colonel Mendonca of being "trigger happy", claiming he once held his pistol over a prisoner's mouth and threatened to "blow his face off". Payne also claimed that he saw Lieutenant Craig Rodgers pretend to set fire to a detainee by setting a jerry can of petrol in front of a young boy, pour water over him and then light a match.

Sri Lankan War Crimes

1983–2009

On 11th November 2013 there were calls for the British Prime Minister, David Cameron, to boycott the Commonwealth summit because of the Sri Lankan government's human rights record. However, it was reported that David Cameron would still attend the Commonwealth summit in Sri Lanka despite India and Canada boycotting the event. The gathering in mid-November 2013 was thrown into turmoil with several members of the Commonwealth refusing to take part. Indian Prime Minister Manmohan Singh followed Canada's Stephen Harper by announcing he would be staying away. The decision put Cameron under fresh pressure to pull out of the Commonwealth Heads of Government Meeting (CHOGM), which was also to be attended by Prince Charles. But Foreign Secretary William Hague said Britain would have "more impact" by raising concerns within the country. Cameron had pledged to put "serious questions" to the Sri Lankan President, Mahinda Rajapaksa, about his regime's widely condemned human rights record and allegations of war crimes against the Tamil minority. Hague said: "We have decided that if we were to stay away it would damage the Commonwealth without changing things positively in Sri Lanka. Sri Lanka is in the spotlight so let's make full use of it being in the spotlight. Rather than sit in

London and talk about it, we will be there. The Prime Minister will be the first head of government from any country since Sri Lankan independence in 1948 to go to the north. It will make more impact in Sri Lanka with the Prime Minister and me there doing that, than sitting in our offices in London."

The UN high commissioner for human rights, Navi Pillay, warned that Sri Lanka – considered a "country of concern" by the Foreign Office – was heading in an "increasingly authoritarian direction". The Sri Lankan government denied allegations that it has been complicit in kidnappings, torture and other abuses amid mounting concerns over "disappearances" and attacks on the judiciary and press. Shadow Foreign Secretary Douglas Alexander said: "In light of reports that the Indian Prime Minister is now considering joining the Canadian Prime Minister in not attending CHOGM because of concerns over human rights, David Cameron must now urgently consider reversing his decision to attend the summit in Sri Lanka this week. The government's policy has descended into confusion following reports that David Cameron assured Tamil representatives that he would consider downgrading Britain's presence at the summit. If the Prime Minister is still refusing to consider downgrading the British delegation, despite reports to the contrary, he must now explain this decision given other Commonwealth leaders are prepared to take a different approach. For months Labour has urged the government to do more to raise Britain's concern over human rights in Sri Lanka in the run up to the summit. If the Prime

Minister now choses to reverse his decision to attend the summit – even at this late stage – he would have Labour's full support."

Religion was at the heart of the problem. The Tamil minority was predominantly Hindu, while the native Sinhalese were Buddhist. During British rule, many poor Tamils were encouraged to emigrate from India to what was then called Ceylon to work on the tea plantations. However, after the Second World War, Tamils became better educated and began to take important jobs in teaching and the civil service as well as in business. But the Sinhalese – who had always held the real political clout – refused to allow any Tamil power-sharing, not even a measure of self-government in the north and east of the island where the majority of Tamils lived. In 1983 hard-line Tamils decided to resort to guns instead of negotiating. In four years 2,500 people had died. The Tamil Tigers were known for their ruthless atrocities, and they wiped out other Tamil factions to become the dominant political force in the area, totally committed to setting up a separate Tamil state in Sri Lanka. Civil war broke out, with both sides guilty of committing terrible atrocities. Many peaceful Tamils found themselves sandwiched between the ferocious Tigers and government forces. By 1987, more than 100,000 Tamils had spent fortunes or risked their lives in open boats trying to escape to safer countries.

In July 1983, more than 3,000 Britons were trapped on a holiday island ravaged by civil war. Most were virtually prisoners in their hotels overlooking the Indian Ocean. A strict dawn-to-4 pm curfew was imposed in Sri Lanka on 27th July following the deaths of 200 people in a wave of rioting, burning and looting. As troops battled to restore order, the British High Commission in the capital, Colombo, warned other holidaymakers to stay at home. Despite this, planes were still leaving Gatwick airport bound for Colombo. The violence in Sri Lanka followed racial clashes between sections of the 12-million-strong Sinhalese population and the 3.5 million Tamils, who wanted a separate state. It dramatically worsened with the massacre of 35 Tamil prisoners in retaliation for the earlier killing of 13 soldiers by Tamil guerillas. Ian Ritchie from Winchester, who managed to board a flight back to Britain, said: "Gangs were roaming the street setting buildings on fire. There were clouds of smoke everywhere." Three years later, more than 200 villagers, including a nine-month-old baby, were burned and shot by Tamil guerillas in a raid in north central Sri Lanka in May. The following month, on 13th June 1986, 47 Tamils were killed when troops stormed a village and fired on three buses. In April 1987 rebels massacred 122 holidaymakers and wounded 60 others when they ambushed three buses and two trucks. Screaming women and children were dragged off the vehicles and mown down with machine guns and grenades. Tamil terrorists then robbed the dead and wounded before fleeing. The government ceasefire was called off as troops were ordered to track down the killers. Most of the victims had been heading home to Colombo after spending local New Year celebrations with relatives.

Tourists avoided Sri Lanka in their droves in the mid-1980s. The palms still swayed in the breeze and the Indian Ocean still lapped lazily along the white sandy beaches, but this was no heaven. It was war-torn and ravaged, with an overbearing sense of menace hanging heavily in the air. Butchery and bloodshed had truly reached paradise. In the week prior to mid-April 1987, nearly 500 people had been slaughtered and hundreds more injured in what was the latest flare-up in the savage civil war that was ripping the country apart. Over the Easter weekend, the Tamil Tigers had shot down 127 men, women and children. A massive car bomb had exploded in the days following at the main bus depot in Colombo as office workers returned home. More than 200 died and 300 were injured. In retaliation, the Sri Lankan government ordered their meager air force to bomb the main Tamil town of Jaffna, killing 80 people. The Easter massacres left a former holiday island in despair.

The car bomb led to troops killing more than 400 Tamil guerillas during a five-day offensive, but two months later, 18 more people were killed when a landmine was set off under a bus in Trincomalee. A second landmine killed a further 13 people in an army convoy – 10 of whom were Tamil prisoners about to be set free having been cleared of terrorist activity. In November 1987 up to 100 people were feared dead after a giant car bomb went off during rush hour in Colombo. In February two years later in 1989, Tamil rebels shot and hacked to death 34 people, including 20 children, in a village in northeast Sri Lanka.

More was to come. Tiger terrorists shot and hacked 127 people to death in attacks on four villages in October 1992. In 2001, Tamil Tiger suicide squads stormed a military base close to the country's main airport. The six-hour blitz left 20 dead and 13 aircraft destroyed. British holidaymakers who were flying home from the Maldives were caught in the cross-fire and very lucky to survive. In 2008, a female suicide bomber blew herself up as she left a train in February. It was the second suspected attack by Tamil Tiger rebels that day. Earlier, on 3rd February, four visitors were injured by a crude explosive device at a zoo. A suicide bomber killed the country's highways minister and 12 others at a marathon race near Colombo on 6th April 2008, and the following month eight were killed in a train blast when a bomb exploded on a busy train during rush hour. In April 2009 a raid on Tamil territory was said to have killed up to 1,000 people. However, the following month the 26-year-old civil war looked as if it would come to an end when Tamil rebels declared a ceasefire.

When David Cameron visited Sri Lanka in November 2013, he was hailed as a "god" by relatives of Sri Lankan war victims. The Prime Minister faced emotional scenes after becoming the first world leader in almost 70 years to visit the island's conflict-ravaged north. He and his entourage were surrounded by distraught family members waving pictures of lost loved ones. They claimed his visit was like "a divine intervention which had given them new hope". They begged him to help them find out what happened to their sons and husbands who had "disappeared" after 26 years of bloody civil war. Hundreds of Sri Lankans, mainly mothers and widows, broke through police security lines to try to speak to Cameron after he arrived in Jaffna, where 40,000 civilians were slaughtered in the last few months of the war, which ended in 2009. The Conservative Party leader was given a hero's welcome as he went to visit Sabapathopillaia refugee camp. The camp's deputy leader, Sutharshan Uthayaswriyan, described the Prime Minister as "a god coming down to this area". He added: "We believe he can make a difference. He is a god and he is sent by God to us." Cameron said: "I think coming here, listening to these people, helps to draw attention to their plight." His comments about Sri Lanka's appalling human rights record were clear. Whether there will be any war criminals brought to justice is yet to be seen.

Sierra Leone and Liberia

1991–2003

With the civil war in Sierra Leone having been ongoing for eight years, the wider world was given a shocking insight in July 1999 when journalist Anton Antonowicz filed his report from the war-torn African country. By the time the conflict ended in 2002, an estimated 50,000 people had lost their lives.

"An 11-year-old boy raises his rifle and becomes a man" reported the *Daily Mirror*. "The Kalashnikov AK47 is his equaliser. He is a child soldier, a child in arms. There are 300,000 children like Felix Musa around the world. They are used because the new nature of war feeds off them. War where civilians, not soldiers, die first. War which demands children in the front line.

"Children are nimble, obedient. They do not insist on pay. They do not have adult responsibilities and cares. Many have already lost their parents, brothers and sisters.

"They are dependent for survival on war and their commanders. Many are dependent, too, on the drugs and hocus-pocus they are fed to make them brave. They are the latest, simplest biological weapon."

Felix Musa was a soldier in Sierra Leone in a war that had been raging for eight years. He was recruited to combat an enemy that embraced savagery. An enemy that declared a policy named "no living thing", in which no one was spared, and where butchery, mutilation and rape were standard.

His commanders recruited him to fight fire with fire. The enemy used children so they did too. It was a practice repeated through Africa, Asia, South America and Europe. The Kosovan Liberation army also used child soldiers.

At the end of the 19th century, one civilian died for every eight soldiers during armed conflict. By the end of the 20th century, nine civilians perished for each soldier. During the 1990s more than 2 million children died in war while another 6 million were seriously injured or disabled.

Civilian populations had become the target, rather than armies. The aim was to cow the mass of the people, to break down their lives and ties, to make them bend before ruthless masters. Bend them, or make them run, as Kosovo showed.

Children were often the killers of choice. Take Felix – he, at least, was governed by a code or drugged into murderous obedience. He was a Kamajor, a member of a secret society of traditional hunters who believe that bullets cannot hurt them. When one of them died they believed it must be because he had broken one of the many rules governing their way of war.

They were not allowed to have sex with a woman when they were fighting, but Felix was too young to feel any sexual desires anyway. He was valued as a virgin. It was believed that virgin boys had the best "ju-ju" – the strongest magic – to turn bullets into water.

The Kamajors rose together in defence of their villages when rebels and the Sierra Leone army joined together to oust the democratically-elected government. The hunters went to war with few weapons – ragtag battalions with only their talismans to protect them. They believed that they could disappear at will. They rushed to the front line, instilling fear in the enemy and taking few prisoners. They amassed captured weapons. They were, for want of a better word, winners.

The evidence of rebel atrocity was stamped on the people living in the poorest country in the world. Special camps had been set up for the men, women and children whose arms, legs, ears and lips had been sliced off by the rebels' machetes and cutlasses. There were places for the women and girls who had been gang-raped not once but daily.

The Americans quickly intervened in Kosovo, but in Sierra Leone – a war that involved far more loss of life – they left it to others.

Felix's mother Jamu said that she was proud of what her boy had been doing since the age of nine, and thanked the Good Lord that the child had never been abducted by rebels. "That's how they get their recruits", she added. "They will swoop on a village, kill all the men, rape the women and take the children for their own uses… converting the boys into killers and the girls into sex slaves. Refuse and die."

Worse still, the rebels forced the children to kill their own parents or die. Massacre your family or take a bullet. Destroy the nightmare with a gun and then sail away on a drug-fuelled cloud.

Refugees were huddled beneath the station sign in Waterloo, a town on the way to coastal Freetown. A checkpoint boasted a hand-written sign declaring "Welcome to the Gateway to Hell". A Kamajor boy, 15-year-old Mahomet Foni, guarded the gateway with his pals. Each wielded Kalashnikovs, which, if you didn't pillage them from dead rebels, you could buy for the price of a chicken.

The bulk of the rebels' supplies were believed to have come from neighbouring Liberia, another ramshackle war-devastated nation. Its president, Charles Taylor, was a disciple of Libya's Colonel Gaddafi. He was also a man who loved the good things in life. The Rolls-Royces, Mercedes and basketball court at his mansion testified to that. So did the gleam in his eyes at the mention of Sierra Leone's vast diamond and gold fields. Sierra Leone had mineral deposits, which could have made it one of Africa's richest countries.

Freetown was the location for a UNICEF (United Nations Children's Fund) camp that contained 42 child ex-combatants and 30 girl "camp followers", the youngest of which was four. Lake Camp was once a beachfront hotel, but the beach was now empty save for the skeletons and corpses that lay there, a fraction of the 50,000 who had died in the war. It was home to 10-year-old Ali Camora, who had been a captain with five bodyguards and as many troops.

"We were one of the Small Boys Units" he explained. "You

see, my mother died and my father disappeared. The rebels took me and trained me to shoot. After that, my job was to cut off people's hands, to burn their houses and to kill. I was promoted because I did it well."

Ali also explained that he really liked the red-and-blue tablets they were given with their food, stating "they gave us power, they made us brave", although he did admit to having bad dreams. They were always the same, of the first woman he killed in Freetown running after him shouting, "You killed me!". He remembered the day itself. He had been told to demand 5,000 Leones (about £2) from her. If she resisted, he was to to kill her and anyone else there. She did not have the money. "I blindfolded her, then I set fire to her and her house. She was running around so I shot her. The others – there were five or six of them in the house – died too." When asked what happened to his mother, Ali explained: "I killed her. When the rebels captured me, they said 'Kill her and your brothers and sister or we will kill you'. I had to set fire to our home. I saw them dying inside."

Others fared little better. The UNICEF-backed Camp of the Amputees contained 500 people, including 38-year-old Fiona Conteh cradling her malaria-fevered daughter Damba. The rebels had cut off the mother and daughter's left hands the previous year, telling her "Now you are washing your hands of the government".

Another victim in the camp was two-and-a-half-year-old Memouna Mousari. Rebels sliced away her right arm, cut off her mother and father's hands and killed her grandmother.

Memouna's mother had been forced to hold the child's arm while the soldiers hacked at it. "They were animals" she exclaimed. "There were men, boys and girls. Chop, chop, chop – the sound of the machetes. The light, it flashed on their blades."

A child's life in the army was clearly explained by three boys quizzed by the *Daily Mirror*. Augustin Willis, 15, stated that they killed because otherwise they would die, and claimed he never drank his victims' blood. He had witnessed men doing it, and had seen them eat the hearts and livers of the dead. "I saw soldiers eating human beings" concurred 12-year-old Thomas Hassan. "I remember one of the men they ate. They started with his heart, then his liver, then one of his legs. They cooked the leg. They were hungry."

Murray Amera was 10 years old and had been a soldier since he was seven. He admitted enjoying shooting people, saying "I was happy when I killed because they were the enemy. There were women and children, but they were the enemy too. I deserted because I'd heard my parents were here. But I can't find them. I don't know what I shall do. All I know is that one day I want to be a doctor. Did I drink any human blood? Of course. We all did. Not many of the boy soldiers were allowed to eat people but we all drank blood."

Just two years later, torture victim Issa Kamara was flown into Britain for an operation that would change his life. The 10-year-old suffered appalling injuries after rebels in Sierra Leone roasted him over a fire. They raped his mother Mabinty and made her sing and clap as she was forced to watch her son being tortured. Issa was due to meet doctors who would repair his burned face and carry out the corrective surgery so he could use his damaged right hand again. "I was afraid" recalled Issa of his ordeal. "I thought they wanted to cook me like a fish and eat me. When I was in the flames, burning, I thought I would soon be dead. I had no hope." Thankfully, Issa was able to put his ordeal behind him and begin some semblance of normality again.

By June 2003, reports were being received that the former ruler of Sierra Leone had been killed. Johnny Paul Koroma died in Liberia, and was believed to have been executed by soldiers of its president, Charles Taylor, who was wanted by the United Nations for genocide. Koroma, leader of the notorious West Side Boys who kidnapped 11 British soldiers in 2000, was responsible for many deaths during the brutal civil war. It was later found that he was not dead – he had gone into hiding.

The following month, rebel leaders in Liberia ordered their forces to stop their onslaught on the capital Monrovia amid claims that 600 civilians had been killed in days of non-stop fighting. President Charles Taylor repeated demands for a peacekeeping force to "bring sanity" to the country ravaged by civil war. A rebel spokesman said "we have given instructions to our forces to stop the fighting".

Heavy gunfire had earlier rung out as battles raged across the city, yet with the streets littered with dead and dying, Taylor still found time to attend his mother's funeral. Weeping, he said:

"Bombs are raining while some members of the international community turn a blind face. They are part of the conspiracy in killing our people."

The US was under pressure to intervene, but President Bush had said that he would send troops only after Taylor, who was wanted for alleged war crimes, resigned. Charles Taylor finally bowed to international pressure in August 2003 and went into exile after standing down as President of Liberia. The former warlord – blamed for 14 years of suffering in the West African state – was defiant to the end. Arriving hours late for his long-promised resignation ceremony, he said history would judge him kindly. Wearing a white safari suit, he stated: "I have accepted this role as sacrificial lamb... I am the whipping boy." He then accused America of backing his enemies, warning: "I leave you with these parting words – God willing, I will be back." The 53-year-old leader handed power to his vice-president, Moses Blah, an old friend and brother-in-arms from his days of bush wars and training in Libya's guerilla training camps. The previous night, rebels who had been besieging the shell-ravaged capital Monrovia for months declared that "war is over". They were unhappy with Blah as Taylor's successor, but West African leaders said an interim government would take over in mid-October.

The televised swearing-in ceremony was attended by South African President Thabo Mbeki. He got a standing ovation after telling the crowds: "It is indeed a shameful thing that, as Africans, we have killed ourselves for such a long time. It is indeed time that this war should come to an end."

Taylor, who had been indicted for war crimes in neighbouring Sierra Leone, was believed to have taken up an offer of asylum in Nigeria. Since he invaded Liberia in 1989, at least 200,000 had been killed in the two civil wars. Within two hours of his departure, three US warships appeared on the horizon. The Americans had been urged by the UN and African nations to take a peacekeeping role, but had been waiting for Taylor to go before moving in.

By June 2006 Britain was offering to lock up Charles Taylor for life if he was convicted of war crimes. The former Liberian president was accused of directing rebels during the Sierra Leone civil war, and faced trial at The Hague. In January 2008, the war crimes trial heard how child soldiers were ordered to mutilate 101 massacred civilians. Churchman Alex Teh said: "After the rebel commander killed them he ordered the Small Boy Units to decapitate them." Two months later, Taylor's alleged Death Squad boss Joseph Marzah explained that cannibalism "was to set an example for the people to be afraid". The war crimes trial heard how opponents and peacekeeping forces were cooked and eaten by the militia of Charles Taylor and that nothing was done without his approval. The former Liberian president denied 11 counts of war crimes and crimes against humanity.

Charles Taylor had come to power in Liberia after a bloody seven-year civil war. After seizing power in 1990, his forces killed, abducted, raped and mutilated civilians. Children would see their families murdered, then be trained as killers. The flamboyant warlord started working with brutal rebel groups in Sierra Leone, supplying weapons in return for "blood diamonds" mined by slave labourers. Taylor went on to win 75 per cent of the vote in a rigged election in 1997 with his supporters reportedly chanting: "He killed my ma, he killed my pa, I'll vote for him."

Taylor was eventually forced to flee, but was captured on the Nigeria–Cameroon border in 2006 with sackfuls of cash by a team working for the UN-backed Special Court for Sierra Leone.

In 2012, Taylor – once one of Africa's most vicious tyrants – became the first ex-head of state to be convicted by an international war crimes court since the Second World War. He was handed a 50-year prison sentence for his part in numerous war crimes and crimes against humanity by the UN-backed court.

The Bosnian War

1992-1995

On 21st December 2011 a woman wanted in Bosnia was arrested over war crimes that were so brutal she was dubbed the "Female Monster". The suspect, named Monika Ilic, was said to have struck fear into her victims, and was accused by one of using a broken bottle to tear open a man's stomach. Monika Ilic's once-childlike appearance is alleged to have hid a cruel streak that she used to the full during the 1992–95 Bosnian war. She was 18 when she married Goran Jelisic, a convicted murderer and concentration-camp torturer. The two allegedly committed crimes against imprisoned non-Serbs in Brčko.

Jelisic, who called himself the "Serb Adolf" after Adolf Hitler, was sentenced in 2001 to 40 years in jail by a United Nations war crimes tribunal. But Ilic evaded justice for years, apparently living in Serbia under a false name for a time. Following an international warrant, police tracked her down in Prijedor, Bosnia, where her boyfriend, Nebojsa Stojanov, lived. She joined just a handful of women who have been accused of or stood trial for war crimes in Bosnia. The most prominent one – and the only former resident of the famous Sheveningen detention unit attached to the UN war crimes tribunal in The Hague – was a former member of the wartime Bosnian Serb leadership, Biljana Plavsic. As one of the creators of the Serb mini-state in Bosnia during the 1992–95 war, she was sentenced by the tribunal in 2003 of persecution, a crime against humanity, as part of an ethnic-cleansing campaign to drive Bosniaks and Croats out of Serb-controlled areas of Bosnia. Plavsic was released in 2009 after serving two-thirds of her 11-year sentence, and then settled in Belgrade. A few years prior to Ilic's arrest, her brother, Konstantin Simonovic, was sentenced to six years for crimes committed as commander of the notorious camp "Luka" where both Ilic and Jelisic are alleged to have operated.

"The anguished faces of the orphans flown out of Sarajevo... touched the heartstrings of the world" wrote the *Daily Mirror* in August 1992. "Those haunted, staring eyes had seen so much horror. Will those children ever recover from the terror of snipers' bullets raking the bus taking them to safety – an attack which left two babies dying amid pools of blood and piles of shattered glass?" The article continued: "Yet, for all their ordeals, those who escaped are the lucky ones. They have left the slaughterhouse that once was Yugoslavia." Thousands of other youngsters were still trapped in the vicious savagery. There was atrocity after atrocity in the war-torn country, which had once been so friendly that millions flocked there for their holidays. It wasn't a nation with a single people bound together by hundreds of years of history; Yugoslavia was arbitrarily created by the Great Powers after the First World War. It was a deadly cocktail of different nationalities, languages and religions. Its people had no common aim. What they did have, wrote the *Daily Mirror*'s foreign editor,

Mark Dowdney, "is hatred for each other". The Serbs and the Croats had always been at each others' throats, he stated. Their vendettas and feuds went back hundreds of years. After 1945 the country was held together by force of arms and the personal power of Marshal Tito. When he died, Yugoslavia began its inevitable slide into anarchy. Local politicians saw their chance to grab control by whipping up nationalist feelings, and no one did so more cynically than Serb leader Slobodan Milošević. His vision of a greater Serbia was what inspired his countrymen to seize huge tracts of land from the Croats and the Muslims. Every acre of the Serbs' shameful prize was stained with blood. More than 10,000 people died in Croatia in 1991, and in 1992 in Bosnia the death toll was a similar number. A horrified Europe watched as concentration camps were once again erected within its borders. There were growing reports of torture and murder in detention camps set up by the Serbs as they went about their so-called "ethnic cleansing" of the territory they snatched. Thousands of civilians were feared to have been killed amid appalling brutality. The first survivors of the death camps told of regular beatings, mass executions and prisoners being starved. Croatia and Bosnia claimed the Serbs ran 45 camps holding at least 70,000 people. The Serbs said that 40,000 of their people were held in Muslim and Croat camps. Fear of falling into the hands of the warring factions created a tidal wave of refugees that threatened to swamp neighbouring countries. More than 2 million people were believed to have fled their homes. The misery they endured to keep their families together and to survive was "impossible to describe" said Dowdney. Most fled north towards Central Europe, but hundreds of thousands were trapped in the former holiday resorts of the Adriatic coast. The reality was that most would never see their homes again. The Serbs swore they would never give up the land they had taken. As the crisis grew, it was also feared that bordering countries would be "sucked in" to the growing conflict. Turkey was furious at the treatment of Muslims in Bosnia and wanted armed intervention to stop the Serbs. Hungary could not cope with the large numbers of displaced people who poured across its borders, and the seeming lack of will by the world's political leaders to take any effective initiatives didn't help either. President Bush's stance in Washington was under increasing attack for his attitude to "a Europe problem". The world's indifference did not go unnoticed by the Serbs, but the UN proved powerless to keep the peace and took far too long to organize relief supplies.

It was reported in August 1982 that thousands of beaten and starving prisoners were moved out of Bosnian concentration camps before the Red Cross was allowed to inspect the sites. The prisoners were secretly packed on to Nazi-style death trains and lorries and shipped to remote areas. A top American official said that they had evidence the Serbs were moving prisoners to fool the Red Cross. The charity's chief feared that the captives had been killed in mass executions, or had died from beatings or the stifling heat of the wagons. Between 2,000 and 4,000 prisoners from Keraterm, a notorious camp set up in a brick factory in Prijedor, were unaccounted for. Keraterm was then closed. Conditions were far worse than in Omarska, where the prisoners were filmed by ITN. Men in another camp told of three mass executions at Keraterm. On each occasion about 200 prisoners were driven to a field. They were made to dig their own graves before being gunned down and killed.

In December 1992, America called for Serb leaders and their battlefront butchers to face war-crime trials. Secretary of State Lawrence Eagleburger blamed Serbia's President Milošević and Bosnia's Serb leader Radovan Karadžić for atrocities in the vicious war in Bosnia. Eagleburger told a Geneva conference that concentration-camp commanders accused of massacres and torture should also be tried. Meanwhile, it was revealed that the Pentagon was drawing up plans to hit air and army bases in a bid to halt the war, but a Pentagon official said that no action would be taken without UN authorization.

On 12th March 1993 trapped British troops escaped from a Bosnian village after Serb guns shelled Muslim women and children, killing at least 16. The 11 soldiers, escorting a UN convoy sent to pick up wounded people, were held hostage for 24 hours by thousands of refugees. Women lay on the road to stop them leaving – and one gave birth as the hostage situation progressed. However, at dawn, the Serbs began shelling the refugees and at least six children under the age of five were injured – two had their legs blown off. Simon Mardell led the troops' medics in emergency surgery without anaesthetic. Major Martin Waters said that the firing was "deliberately" aimed at women and children. The following month, British troops were close to tears as they walked through a village massacre in which all 400 inhabitants were feared dead. They found only charred bodies in the village of Ahinici in the Bosnian mountains. There was no sign of life. Every house was burned out. Even dogs and farm animals had been shot. In one house, at least six members of one family were found shot or burned to death. Two bodies in the hallway appeared to be a father and son. The remains of a mother and three or four children were found in the cellar.

Radovan Karadžić was unveiled as "the unacceptable face of the Serbs, a shameless stooge for the perpetrators of some of the worst atrocities in Europe". He flew around the world telling barefaced lies as his countrymen continued to massacre women and children. However, the president of the Bosnian Serbs wasn't able to keep talking himself out of trouble. He had to face parliament and his own hard-line MPs, who were furious that he signed the Vance-Owen peace plan after 12 hours of arm-twisting talks in Athens. Many of them considered it a total betrayal of what they had been fighting for. By force of arms and appalling cruelty, Serb forces had captured 70 per cent of Bosnia. Under the Vance-Owen plan, they were supposed to give almost half of it back to the Croats and Muslims. It was thought that Milošević would dump Karadžić.

More atrocities came in June 1993 when 50 patients and

staff were killed at a hospital in Bosnia that had been shelled by Serbs. There were no survivors when the temporary medical centre took a direct hit as Serb gunners pounded the town of Goražde. In August 1995, 40 civilians were slaughtered in a Sarajevo market. An old man wept as the shell-shattered bodies of men, women and children lay on the ground. Shards of red-hot shrapnel scythed through the teeming crowds at the entrance to the covered market on Titova Street in Sarajevo. Toddlers, children, mums, dads and the elderly were all torn down. More than 90 people were wounded, some critically, while dead victims were draped over steel railings and body parts littered the ground amid pools of blood. One old man lay dead, still astride his ancient motorcycle, his head split apart. The air was filled with the screams of the wounded and dying and the wails of relatives and friends. A girl aged about five cried in terror and shock: "Mummy, I've lost my hand." She was rushed to hospital in the back of a passing car, clutching her shattered arm in a blood-soaked blanket. Her mother lost an eye in the blast. Amid worldwide outrage, action was ordered by UN Secretary-General Boutros Boutros-Ghali, and NATO warplanes were poised to hit back hard. At last, it was decided that the Serbs could not be allowed to get away with mass murder.

Meanwhile, in 1997, terrified Serb warlord Karadžić hid behind 500 troops. He was convinced that he was the next SAS target after Simo Drljaca had been shot dead. By this time Karadžić had been twice indicted for genocide and was to face trial in The

Hague. Milošević, however, earned his place in history's Hall of Infamy as the man responsible for the most appalling atrocities in Europe. His whole career had been devoted to power, and his chief weapon was treachery. He revelled in collecting files on everyone around him, knowing that no one had much on him. Both his parents had committed suicide and his wife's mother had been shot by the Nazis, so neither had a settled past. Filled with dark memories, he showed he was capable of sacrificing hundreds of thousands of people in a war without compassion. He was a man ready to step on bodies in his pathological pursuit of power. All the bloodshed sparked by the then "new man of peace" was unbelievable. Nationalism had been his mainstay, and he had used it on the path to power in 1987. When NATO showered bombs on the Bosnian Serbs in 1996 he abandoned them for his new face as a peacemaker. Western leaders knew he lied and murdered and still they tried to make deals with him. However, in 1999, the threat of air strikes against Serbia grew following the massacre of 45 villagers in Kosovo. The victims were found on a hillside near Račak. Some had their eyes gouged out or their heads smashed. One was decapitated and many had been shot at close range. Serbia had been warned in October 1998 that it faced NATO military action if it broke a ceasefire pledge. Milošević had been forced to withdraw police and troops from the province and a fragile peace was established. Britain, the US, France and Germany protested over the atrocity as NATO leaders met in Brussels to discuss their next move. Meanwhile, war-crimes tribunal judge, Louise Arbour, was due to arrive in Kosovo to investigate the slaughter.

That same month, it was announced that the leaders of Serbia's brutal high command were warned that they would be hunted down and tried for war crimes over the barbarity in Kosovo. Milošević headed the list of seven senior political and military leaders named by British Foreign Secretary Robin Cook as NATO's most wanted men. Intelligence experts said that they were behind at least 25 massacres involving innocent civilians in Kosovo in 13 months. They were also blamed for devising the "new apartheid" that had seen hundreds of thousands of ethnic Albanians driven from their homeland at gunpoint or murdered. Apart from Milošević, those on the wanted list were internal security chief Radomir Marković, Colonel-General Dragolub Ojdanić, Colonel-General Nebojša Pavković and Major-General Vladimir Lazarević.

Nikolai Sainovic, the deputy prime minister, was being closely monitored, as was interior minister Vlajko Stoliljković, in charge of the vicious paramilitary police. United Nations Secretary-General Kofi Annan spoke for the world on the horror of the Kosovo tragedy on why babies, children, women and men should have the right to live without persecution. His moving address to a Geneva human rights commission in April 1999 was the strongest testament yet to back the UN's stand against ethnic cleansing. In his closing statement he said: "Let me be very clear: even though we are an organization of Member States, the rights and ideals the United Nations exists to protect are those of peoples." In July 2001, Milošević was driven through Belgrade to face justice for war crimes. He was handed over to UN officials to stand trial in The Hague.

On 2nd August 2001, General Radislav Krstić was sentenced to 46 years after the first genocide conviction by a UN war crimes tribunal. The 94-day trial heard witnesses tell of mass murder, decapitations and torture. Judge Almiro Rodrigues told Krstić: "You are guilty of genocide. You are guilty of inflicting incredible suffering." Meanwhile, Milošević's wife said there was an international conspiracy to "nail him for war crimes". Known as the "Red Witch of Belgrade", she insisted that her husband was innocent of the crimes of which he was accused. He himself said the charges were absurd. On 11th March 2006, he was found dead in his cell in the UN war crimes tribunal detention centre. While some believed he died of a heart attack, others believed he had been murdered.

Rwanda Genocide

1994

On 18th December 2008 Theoneste Bagosora, 67, was found guilty of leading a committee of extremists who plotted mass deaths 14 years earlier. As Rwanda's defence chief, he then ordered Hutu soldiers to go on the 100-day massacre. Goaded by hate messages from the Hutu government in 1994, militias went from village to village slaughtering men, women and children. Hundreds of thousands of ethnic Tutsis and moderate Hutus were butchered. Bagosora was also behind the deaths of former Prime Minister Agathe Uwilingiyimana and 10 Belgian peacekeepers. General Romeo Dallaire, head of UN peacekeepers at the time, described Mr Bagosora as the "kingpin behind the genocide". On 18th December 2008 a UN tribunal sitting in Tanzania found him guilty of instigating the genocide. Jean Paul Rurangwa, 32, who lost his father and two sisters, said: "The fact he was sentenced to the biggest punishment the court can give is a relief."

Ex-commanders Anatole Nsengiyumva and Aloys Ntabakuze also got life in jail after being found guilty of genocide. The tribunal had, at this point, convicted 34 people, but Bagosora was set to appeal against the verdict. Then, in May 2011, an army thug who ordered the deaths of thousands of innocent Rwandans was jailed for 30 years. A former general, Augustin Bizimungu was said to have supplied militants with weapons to murder ethnic Tutsi tribespeople, who he branded "cockroaches". The brutal 59-year-old also provided fuel for the marauding gangs to burn down homes. He was jailed after being convicted of ordering attacks during the 1994 genocide that left 800,000 Tutsis and moderate Hutus dead. A Rwanda war crimes court held in neighbouring Tanzania heard Bizimungu had full control over the men he commanded. Chief prosecutor Martin Ngoga said: "It is a welcome decision. It is a big sentence, even if many people think he deserved the highest." Bizimungu showed no emotion as he was locked up. Former police chief Augustin Ndindiliyimana was also convicted over his role in the genocide, but he was released as he had already served time. Two other generals were each jailed for 20 years for taking part in the 100-day killing spree, which had been sparked by the death of President Juvenal Habyarimana who had been shot down in a plane on 6th April 1994. Government officials organized Hutu militias across the country to systematically kill Tutsis, who they blamed for the assassination.

On 24th June 2011, a former Rwandan government minister became the first woman ever to be convicted of genocide. A former minister for family and women's affairs, Pauline Nyiramasuhuko ordered the massacre and rape of women and girls. Her son Arsene Ntahobali, a former militia leader, was found guilty of the same crimes by the UN-backed court for Rwanda, who were trying suspects after the 1994 atrocities in which mostly ethnic Tutsis were killed. The pair had helped Hutu extremists abduct Tutsis, who were assaulted, raped and killed in the African country's southern Burate region.

The judgment read by the presiding judge, William Sekule, said: "During the course of these repeated attacks on vulnerable civilians, both Nyiramasuhuko and Ntahobali ordered killings. They also ordered rapes. Ntahobali further committed rapes and Nyiramasuhuko aided and abetted rapes." Both mother and son were jailed for life along with a former mayor, Elie Ndayambaje. The judgments came 10 years after trials at the International Criminal Tribunal for Rwanda, based in neighbouring Tanzania, began and 16 years after some of the accused were arrested. Though Nyiramasuhuko is the first woman to be convicted of genocide, former Bosnian Serb leader Biljana Plavsic faced the same charge in 2000 but it was dropped as part of a plea bargain that saw her admit crimes against humanity. She was jailed for 11 years but was released in 2009.

It was reported on 16th April 1994 that more than 650 children and 500 adults sheltering in war-torn Rwanda had been massacred. They died as soldiers kicked open the doors and opened up with automatic rifles before throwing in grenades. Then the troops moved in with knives, bats and spears, clubbing anyone left alive in the town of Musha, 25 miles from the capital, Kigali. The atrocity was revealed by a Croatian missionary in charge of the local church. Pastor Danko Litrick said: "The soldier broke in at 6.30 am. Afterwards there were 1,180 bodies in my church, including 650 children." He and another priest had been forced to run for their lives and hide. A huge pile of bodies was reported to be still in the church following the massacre. Many of them had been hacked to pieces. Polish Roman Catholic missionaries then reported a second massacre inside a church. They said that a mob armed with machetes and grenades had killed about 80 men, women and children at a church in Kigali. "You could hear the machetes cutting and the moans and calls for help" said the Reverend Henryk Pastuszka. Fighting and tribal bloodshed had ravaged Rwanda for a week at this point, and thousands of Westerners, including up to 100 Britons, had been evacuated to safety. At least 30,000 people were believed to have died up to this point. The bloodletting raged on unchecked as government troops and rebels fired rockets and mortars in the days of fighting for control of Kigali. The UN tried to negotiate a ceasefire as an eight-mile-long column of refugees poured out of the corpse-strewn capital. Around 100,000 people were thought to have fled the city on foot. A UN official said: "There are hundreds of thousands in the city cut off from anything decent or human. People and babies are starving to death. People are in hiding and cannot find food. Hospitals are not functioning." More than 14,000 people were seeking shelter at UN secure positions at Kigali's main King Faisal Hospital and a nearby stadium, but a UN spokesman warned that it was not equipped to protect them. "We are feeding people and looking after them as best we can" he said. "We are running convoys to the airport and responding to requests to evacuate foreign nationals." But he added that the city had descended into lawlessness. Armed gangs were roaming the streets looting and attacking everyone they met. Tutsi rebels had warned the UN to complete the evacuation of foreigners by a deadline. Anyone who remained after that time would be treated as hostile.

In May 1994 victims of the Rwanda bloodbath faced a stark choice – buy a bullet for a quick end or be hacked to death. The choice was revealed to French Health Minister Philippe Douste-Blazy by a 20-year-old Tutsi woman who had been left for dead by her attackers. She said that Hutu militiamen told their victims: "If you can pay, we will kill you with a Kalashnikov, otherwise we'll use machetes." The minister told a French TV station that 200,000 to 500,000 people had been killed "in the worst genocide in the 20th century". Children were deliberately not spared. Radio Uganda broadcast that up to 40,000 corpses had floated into Lake Victoria.

"Patrice is lying dead in the dirt, arms open, one hand raised, one finger pointing forwards" reported the *Daily Mirror* in July 1994. Next to him, beneath him and over him lay the trampled corpses of 38 other children. Looters had picked their way through this mass of rags and tangled tragedy. A huddle of abandoned babies crawled screaming in the dirt nearby. It was just 22 hours since the children had been trampled, yet no one came to take the dead or care for the tiny survivors in the shadow of the high walls of Muzizi's primary school. The Red Cross were on their way, but their progress was slow through the thousands of refugees crawling across the border. Patrice and the other children had died in what they thought was safety. They had crossed the border, which stood like a savage joke 50 yards from where they were lying. Fear and hatred had brought them to their resting place, driving them and 1.5 million other refugees away from their homes. Patrice's identity card said that he was a Hutu – the majority tribe who fled after murdering more than half a million Tutsis. The Tutsi forces – by this time in power in a country half the size of Wales – had pushed the boy and his parents into Zaire. The Rwandan army, and militiamen then threw grenades at them as a parting gift to the Rwandan Patriotic Front (RPF). The children died as a result.

In another attack, a four-year-old girl lay decapitated. There were another 30 bodies strewn around her. The plight of the refugees made aid work almost impossible. There wasn't enough water, let alone food, and the relief agencies were ordered to think of their own personal safety first. The *Daily Mirror* reporter who found Patrice eventually found the four-year-old Tuyisinge lying attached to a drip dying of dysentery in a Médecins Sans Frontières dispensary. The orderlies had just one plastic bottle left with 500 quinine tablets for malaria, but there were 60,000 people outside in desperate need of help. The 1.5 million refugees needed 7 million litres of water each day. The *Daily Mirror*'s journalist, finding Filippo Grandi, the UNHCR boss, at the airport where he was waiting to greet President Clinton's adviser Brian Attwood, reported: "It is a catastrophe. A defeat for humanity." Elsewhere, in a French military tent two teams of surgeons were clocking their 20th hour at the operating table.

Shrapnel-torn children and women lay beneath foil blankets while the refugees of Rwanda kept walking towards what they believed to be a safer haven. They marched with fear prodding them in the back towards what they had a faint hope would be refuge.

In Zaire, once refugees reached it, cholera was raging out of control. At least 14,000 people had died in squalid, teeming camps where thousands of corpses were stacked in the open. Aid workers began burning the bodies because they had nowhere else to bury them. A mass grave the size of a football pitch was filled on the outskirts of Goma in eastern Zaire. One refugee leading his children out of Zaire said: "We are all dying. It is better to be killed in Rwanda." Just 11 days earlier, in July 1994, there had been a mass exodus of people escaping the killers carrying out appalling massacres, but by the end of the month many were retracing their steps. Brigitte Umera, 16, walked alone. She had escaped with her father and two brothers after militiamen from the former regime murdered her mother. She was a Tutsi tribeswoman. Her father was spared because he was Hutu. The remaining family reached Homa, but the young girl then lost her father and brothers. Alone and traumatized, she was going to trek back 60 miles to her home in the south. She hoped that if her father and brothers were still alive they would find her there.

Somewhere, hidden from the world's eyes, were the bodies of 500,000 Tutsis slaughtered by fleeing militiamen. In the village of Jenda lay the remains of their "work". Homes had been reduced to rubble and clothes were scattered, but there were no bodies. Celest Kabanda, 27, fled from the murderers. His parents, wife and seven brothers and sisters had all died. "They put them in my father's house and then threw grenades through the window" he said. The Tutsis talked of bringing justice to a country after 25 years of military dictatorship, of teaching people brainwashed with ethnic hatred to live and work as one. Hutu Jean Weneymongo, 34, returned from Katale refugee camp. He said at least 50 people from his village had died. But, like others, the conditions in Zaire had forced him back home.

Many believed they no longer needed to fear the RPF, but the killing began again in March 1995. Kigali prison was crammed with prisoners, mostly Hutus, and every square inch was "carpeted" with those accused of genocide. The government was trying to do what it could to bring murderers to book but it had a very long way to go. On 24th April 1998 firing squads brushed aside international protests and executed 22 prisoners convicted of genocide in Rwanda. More than 30,000 people gathered in the capital to watch three men and one woman be tied to posts and shot. Schools were closed so that pupils could attend. Another 18 people were executed in similar gatherings in four main towns, and hundreds more deaths were planned. The doomed were ringleaders of the slaughter in which an estimated 800,000 had died.

However, in 1999, the former Rwandan army chief suspected of massacring 100,000 people had been given refuge in Britain. Lieutenant-Colonel Tharcisse Muvunyi was top of the list of alleged war criminals wanted by the African country's government. The

Home Office had allowed him to set up home in Lewisham, London, with his wife and three teenage children. He was living there on benefits, studying English. The Foreign Office said it was up to the UN's International Criminal Tribunal for Rwanda (UNICTR) to issue a warrant for his arrest. In April 2004, survivors of the genocide buried the remains of victims to mark the 10th anniversary of the slaughter. A total of 20 coffins containing the bones of hundreds shot and hacked to death were lowered into tombs near the capital. President Paul Kagame, whose rebels ended the Tutsi murders by toppling the Hutu rulers, laid a wreath on the 20th coffin.

In 2006, France was blamed for the assassination that sparked the genocide. The President of Rwanda claimed that France also harboured Hutu officials who oversaw the 100-day massacre. France was accused of backing Hutu commanders who shot down the plane of Juvenal Habyarimana after he signed a peace deal with Tutsi rebels. Rwanda then severed diplomatic ties with Paris. In December 2006, four men accused over the genocide were remanded in custody by a London court. They were held following police raids in London, Manchester, Essex and Bedfordshire. At the same time it emerged that Britain could have been harbouring up to 100 Rwandans suspected of atrocities. The four men were Vincent Bajinya (also known as Vincent Brown), Charles Munyaneza, Celestin Ugirashebuja and Emmanuel Nteziryayo. All the men were accused of extremely heinous war crimes. Bagosora was eventually jailed for life for leading the extremists and for plotting mass killings.

The War in
Afghanistan

2001–

As darkness fell outside the chapel of rest at Camp Bastion in January 2010, the coffin of *Daily Mirror* defence correspondent Rupert Hamer was draped in the Union flag. It was an honour reserved normally only for military personnel, but such was the respect that Rupert had earned from those he lived and died alongside, the rules were quietly pushed aside to give a civilian a real military send-off. It was the ultimate accolade for a reporter as devoted to the brave men and women of the armed forces as he was to reporting the realities of life on the front line. "We gave him a fantastic send off" said a close military friend of Rupert, who asked to remain anonymous. He had seen Rupert three times in just over a month – in London in early December, two weeks later in Camp Bastion and just after New Year in Kabul. Their friendship had been forged two years before in the battle heat of Musa Qala. The friend had never dreamed it would end like this. "It was a day that I hoped would never come. I spent 10 to 15 minutes alone with [Rupert's] coffin, paying my respects. It was good to have a bit of time and space with him, thinking about the last few times we met. I was able to pay my proper respects to a really down-to-earth bloke who never wrote any bullshit."

Just after 1.00 am, Rupert's plaque-engraved casket, covered in the Union flag, was carried by pallbearers on to the chilly desert airstrip. The "ramp ceremony" was held on the tarmac next to the C-130 transporter plane that was to bring home the bodies of Rupert and 19-year-old Private Robert Hayes, of 1st Battalion The Royal Anglian Regiment, who had been killed by a roadside bomb a few days earlier.

"It was the most fantastic send-off for a non-military person that you could have" said the friend. An army padre led a brief service, watched by the Foreign Office's Lindy Cameron, the most senior British diplomat in Helmand province. As with every one of the 245 military deaths in Afghanistan previously, exactly what was said was kept private. It is the soldier's farewell to their comrades and just as personal in its own way as the family funerals that follow it at home. Prayers were said over the bodies of the two men and a minute's silence was held. Then the pallbearers slowly carried the coffins into the C-130.

"The view was taken that they wanted to pay Rupert exactly the same respect as they do for soldiers" a senior army source said. "It is a sensitive issue because British civilians killed abroad, even in a war, do not normally have these rites. But it was felt, in Rupert's case, that the rules should be broken."

The previous Saturday, on the 9th of January 2010, Rupert had become the first British journalist to die in the Afghanistan conflict while on a patrol with soldiers of the 1st Battalion, 3rd US Marine Corps, with whom he and photographer Phil Coburn were embedded. The pair were in the last vehicle in a convoy of Mine-Resistant Ambush Protected (MRAP) personnel carriers, known as Cougars. They were near the town of Nawa when their Cougar was blasted by a roadside bomb at 11.55 am. Medics were unable to save Rupert or US Marine Mark Juarez, 23, who was in the same vehicle. Phil and four other marines were severely injured.

Rupert's body was repatriated, and an inquest into his death opened and adjourned by Wiltshire coroner David Ridley. The inquest was told that Rupert's vehicle was "apparently struck by an improvised explosive device". His interim cause of death was given as "multiple injuries in keeping with the effects of an explosion" and Wiltshire Police investigated his death prior to a full hearing. It was concluded that his death was as a result of a crime.

Father-of-three Rupert had worked for the *Daily Mirror* for over 12 years, the previous five as defence correspondent. It was his sixth visit to Afghanistan. Major-General Tim Cross, second-in-command of the Allied operation to rebuild Iraq post-war, and who had a great respect for Rupert and his work, said the honour bestowed on him by soldiers on the ground was richly deserved. "He may not have worn campaign medals on his chest, but he stands firmly alongside those who do" he said. "Like all those flown home from operations, he will not be forgotten. He and his family have our deep respect and thanks, and his wife and children should be, and I am sure are, enormously proud of him."

However, it wasn't just the Taliban who were carrying out

atrocities. On 8th November 2013, a 39-year-old Royal Marine, Sergeant Alexander Blackman, then known only as "Marine A", was found guilty of murder in front of a military hearing at Bulford, Wiltshire, and on 6th December 2013 he was sentenced to life in prison. Two other marines were cleared of murder after the tribunal heard that Sergeant Blackman had fired the fatal shot into the insurgent's chest. An inquiry would focus on what led to the killing, the atmosphere in Helmand province at that time and whether lessons could be learned. The tribunal ruling was the first time a serviceman had been convicted of a war crime in the 12-year conflict. But, a Ministry of Defence spokesman said: "No decision has yet been made about whether we will hold an inquiry."

In the news the day after the conviction, Prime Minister David Cameron said that the actions of the sergeant who executed the Taliban fighter should not "besmirch" the Royal Marines' proud history. Speaking to a group of serving and former Royal Marines raising cash for the Commando 999 charity outside Downing Street, he said: "That in no way represents the spirit and the history of the Royal Marines, an outfit that has one of the proudest histories of any in the world. We should not let that single incident besmirch the incredible work the Royal Marines have done, not only over decades but over centuries." The Prime Minister said the Royal Marines "leave the country in a far better state than when we found it", with there being "no functioning Afghan state" when they arrived in 2001. He said: "I wanted to say a big thank you to the Royal Marines for the incredible work you have done in Afghanistan over the last decade. I believe we will be able to leave that country with our heads held high."

Meanwhile, a Royal Marines general had called for leniency towards Sergeant Blackman. Major-General Julian Thompson, who led 3 Commando Brigade during the Falklands War, refused to condemn the marine, and told *The Times* that a five-year prison term would be more suitable than life imprisonment. Major-General Thompson said the shorter prison term was more appropriate for a crime committed under the unique pressures of war. He said that "obviously it was wrong and everyone in the Royal Marines is quite clear about that". But he added: "The Royal Marines are a family and it feels as though a member of the family has transgressed. I am sad for the man who did it, in that he probably had a moment of stupidity. I feel for him as I would my own son who might do something stupid." He said that accepting an enemy's surrender on the battlefield was "a very, very dangerous time", adding: "I have no sympathy for the man who was killed but Marine A did the wrong thing by shooting him. But I'm not going to stand around bad-mouthing him. I won't condemn him. It is like a member of the family who has broken the law – you don't reject them, but you support them." Many others, however, did not feel the same. Royal Marine top brass described the execution of a Taliban fighter by a commando as "a truly shocking and appalling aberration". The Deputy Commandant General, Brigadier Bill Dunham, said: "It shouldn't have happened and should never happen again."

The veteran 39-year-old sergeant claimed he had thought the heavily armed enemy soldier was dead and had fired the shot in anger. But a panel of seven servicemen refused to believe him, following a two-week court martial which heard how he had fired a 9mm pistol shot into the seriously injured man's chest at close range. He told fellow marines after shooting the man: "This doesn't go anywhere. I just broke the Geneva Convention." The Helmand killing in September 2011 was recorded on another marine's helmet camera together with audio. The audio recording was released as the judge summed up the evidence at the court martial of the three soldiers originally accused of murder. Royal Marines are heard laughing at a comrade's offer to shoot the wounded Taliban fighter in the head. After finding the seriously hurt enemy soldier lying in a field after an Apache helicopter attack, one soldier says: "I'll put one in his head, if you want." Laughter is heard from others, before Sergeant Blackman says: "No, not in his head, 'cause that'll be f****** obvious." Later a single shot is heard, followed by groans from the man whose name, age and nationality are not known. After the shot is fired, Sergeant Blackman can be heard telling him: "There you are. Shuffle off this mortal coil you c***. It's nothing you wouldn't do to us." The two audio clips were taken from a six-minute video of the marines on patrol in Helmand province on 15th September 2011. Judge Advocate General Jeff Blackett ruled that the accompanying graphic video footage should not be released. He told the court martial that it might be used as propaganda by terror groups. He added: "More importantly to release it would increase the threat of harm to British service personnel." Judge Blackett permitted the issue of 11 stills from the video, captured on the camera worn by one of the marines. They showed the backs of the soldiers but did not feature their alleged victim. The video footage, which was shown to a panel of seven serving servicemen, shows the Royal Marine patrol standing outside a field of tall crops, with an Apache helicopter audible overhead. They can be heard swearing and complaining about their task of carrying out a battle-damage assessment after the Apache attack. During the trial, the court martial heard that the insurgent had been shot at with 139 30mm cannon rounds but that he was still alive, albeit seriously injured, when discovered by the patrol. One marine can be heard asking "Why didn't they use a fucking rocket?" Another replies: "Fuck me, it's just error after error after error." Sergeant Blackman and another marine are then seen scouting out the field, locating the Afghan before calling the others over. The camera shows a shot of the seriously injured insurgent lying on the ground covered in blood. The patrol drags the man across the field and into a wooded area nearby, throwing him to the ground. The injured man, carrying a gun and a grenade, according to the audio transcript, suffers kicks from the servicemen, who then flip him from back to front. Sergeant Blackman is seen to walk forward, bend down and shoot the man in the chest with a 9mm pistol. Giving evidence to the court martial, he insisted that he believed the insurgent was dead at the time and was shooting into a corpse in anger. However, after shooting the man, Sergeant Blackman is seen turning to the other members of the patrol and telling them: "Obviously this doesn't go anywhere fellas." The three marines denied murder and the panel retired to consider verdicts before finding Sergeant Blackman guilty of murder.

As the verdict against Sergeant Blackman was disclosed, the Defence Secretary, Philip Hammond, who was visiting Helmand province, said that no one on deployment in Afghanistan had called for clemency for the sergeant. He said that everyone believed murder was against the values of both Britain and its armed forces. The Defence Secretary's comments echoed the views of General Sir Nicholas Houghton, the Chief of the Defence Staff, who said that the army must be "immaculate" in upholding judicial process. Mr Hammond said: "I have not heard any such suggestions [for clemency] here. People here understand part of what makes us different from the insurgents and the terrorists that we are going after is we maintain a certain standard. These are standards that are core to our values as a society and core to the values of the British Armed Forces. This is an isolated incident, I believe, one individual who has let the side down. It is not indicative of the kind of behaviour that people in the British Armed Forces condone or expect to indulge in. I have heard no suggestion since I have been here [that] there is any request for special treatment for anyone convicted of the crime of murder."

Speaking earlier on the BBC One *Andrew Marr Show*, General Houghton said: "My position on this is no serviceman or woman of the British Armed Forces is above the law – not above the law of the country, international law or the law of armed conflict. This was a heinous crime. Judicial process has found this individual guilty. It would be quite wrong for the armed forces to adopt some special pleading, some sort of exemption. If we try to put ourselves beyond the law or expect special provision from the law, then we start to erode the position where we have a moral ascendancy over those who are our enemies and that is the wrong thing to do. There is a due process that will lead to a sentencing. It's for that process to determine whether or not any form of clemency should be shown in the sentencing... we would not want our position to be eroded. Those in authority over the armed forces should not request any form of leniency... we should be immaculate in these respects. Murder is murder, this is a heinous crime, thankfully it is an exceptional act in terms of the conduct of our armed forces."

Two days before the final verdicts were read out, the terror chief who ordered the murder of schoolgirl Malala Yousafzai was elected as the new leader of the Taliban in Pakistan. The appointment of Mullah Fazlullah, 37, dashed hopes that the fanatics, who want to impose Sharia law in the nuclear-armed nation, might join talks with the government. In 2012, he ordered his men to shoot Malala because she called for education for girls. She miraculously recovered after being airlifted to the UK and now lives in Birmingham with her family. The rise of Fazlullah followed the killing of predecessor Hakimullah Mehsud a week before in a US drone strike in North Waziristan. He was one of Pakistan's most wanted men, with a £3 million US bounty on his head. His second in command was killed in May 2013. Mehsud and his allies had been tentatively considering starting ceasefire talks with the government, but the new chief ruled out any co-operation.

"There will be no more talks as Mullah Fazlullah is already against negotiations with the Pakistan government" Shahidullah Shahid, a Taliban spokesman, told Reuters by telephone from an undisclosed location in neighbouring Afghanistan. "All governments play double games with us. In the name of peace talks, they deceived us and killed our people. We are one hundred per cent sure that Pakistan fully supports the United States in its drone strikes." The spokesman said Fazullah was in full control of the insurgent regime in Pakistan and was deciding whether to avenge the death of Mehsud with a new campaign of bombings and killings. He was believed to be in hiding in the Nuristan province of Afghanistan as of mid-November 2013.

In October 2013, the brave schoolgirl, education campaigner and Pride of Britain winner told of the moment she was shot in the head by the Taliban. The insurgent group may have robbed her of her smile, but they failed to take the one thing they feared the most of this young girl – her spirit. She was a 15-year-old fighting for the right to have an education when she was gunned down on the bus taking her home from lessons. Her miraculous recovery was the start of a journey that took her from her home in a remote Pakistan valley to the UN in New York. She told, in exclusive extracts, published in the *Mirror*, from her new book, how the day "everything changed was Tuesday, October 9, 2012, three months after my 15th birthday. It wasn't the best of days to start with as it was the middle of school exams. But as a bookish girl I didn't mind them as much as some of my classmates did. My classes were spent chanting chemical equations or studying Urdu grammar, writing stories in English with morals like "Haste makes waste" or drawing diagrams of blood circulation – most of my classmates wanted to be doctors. It's hard to imagine that anyone would see that as a threat. Yet outside lay not only the noise and craziness of Mingora, the main city of the Swat Valley in northwest Pakistan, but also those like the Taliban who think girls should not go to school. The school was not far from my home but I had started going by rickshaw and coming back by bus because my mother was scared of me walking on my own. We had been getting threats all year. Some were in the newspapers, some were notes or messages passed on by people. The Taliban had never come for a girl and I was more concerned that they would target my father as he was always speaking out against them. A close friend of his and fellow campaigner had been shot in the face and I knew everyone was telling my father: 'Take care, you'll be next.'

"When our bus was called that afternoon, the other girls all covered their heads before emerging from the door and climbing into the white Toyota van with benches in the back. I sat with my friend Moniba and a girl called Shazia Ramzan, holding our exam folders to our chests and with our school bags under our feet. The bus turned right off the main road at the army checkpoint as always and rounded the corner past the deserted cricket ground. I don't remember any more. But I now know that a young bearded man stepped into the road and waved the van down. As he spoke to the driver another young man approached the back. 'Who is Malala?' he demanded. No one said anything but several of the girls looked at me. I was the only girl with my face not covered. He lifted up a black pistol, a Colt .45. Some of the girls screamed and Moniba tells me I squeezed her hand.

"The man fired three shots. The first went through my left eye socket and out under my left shoulder. I slumped forward on to Moniba, blood coming from my left ear, so the other bullets hit those near to me. One went into Shazia's left hand. The third went through her left shoulder and into the upper right arm of another girl, Kainat Riaz. My friends later told me the gunman's hand was shaking as he fired. By the time we got to the hospital my long hair and Moniba's lap were full of blood. I was rushed to the intensive care unit of the Combined Military Hospital, Peshawar.

"Colonel Junaid, a neurosurgeon, told my father a bone had fractured and splinters had gone into my brain, creating a shock and causing it to swell. He needed to remove some of my skull to give the brain space to expand, otherwise the pressure would become unbearable. 'We need to operate now to give her a chance,' he said. 'If we don't, she may die. I don't want you to look back and regret not taking action.' I woke on October 16, a week after the shooting. The first thing I thought was, 'Thank God I'm not dead.' But I had no idea where I was. I knew I was not in my homeland. The nurses and doctors were speaking English though they all seemed to be from different countries. I didn't know what had happened. The nurses weren't telling me anything. Even my name. But I had been flown to Birmingham.

"My head was aching so much that even the injections they gave me couldn't stop the pain. My left ear kept bleeding and I could feel that the left side of my face wasn't working properly. If I looked at the nurses for too long my left eye watered. I didn't seem to be able to hear from my left ear and my jaw wouldn't move properly. The day my parents flew to Birmingham I was moved into a room with windows. I could look out and see England for the first time. They tried to hide it but I could see my parents were disturbed by how I looked. My father would boast about 'my heavenly smile and laughter'. Now he lamented to my mother, 'That beautiful symmetrical face, that bright shining face has gone; she has lost her smile and laughter. The Taliban are very cruel – they have snatched her smile.' The problem was a facial nerve. The doctors were not sure if it was damaged and might repair itself, or if it was cut. I reassured my mother that it didn't matter if my face was not symmetrical. Me, who had always cared about my appearance, how my hair looked. But when you see death, things change.

"'It doesn't matter if I can't smile or blink properly'," I told her, "I'm still me, Malala. The important thing is God has given me my life." A surgeon called Richard Irving operated on me on November 11. He explained that this nerve's job was to open and close my left eye, move my nose, raise my left eyebrow and make me smile. After three months the left side of my face started working bit by bit. I could soon smile and wink and more movement was coming into my face. An electronic device called a cochlear implant was also placed inside my head near the damaged left ear and I was told I should soon be able to hear. A Taliban fires three shots at point-blank range at three girls and doesn't kill any of them. People prayed to God to spare me and I was spared for a reason – to use my life for helping people."

Days after being shot, Malala was airlifted to the UK where she spent four months receiving treatment at Birmingham's Queen Elizabeth Hospital. After making a remarkable recovery, she was discharged and has since gone on to speak around the world about girls' rights to go to school. During an event in Edinburgh on 19th October 2013, the teenager was reunited with school friends Kainat Riaz and Shazia Ramzan for the first time since the bus attack – and the three vowed they would not be afraid to continue their campaign. The girls all now live and study in the UK. Speaking at the first public meeting of the Global Citizenship Commission – organized in part by former Prime Minister Gordon Brown – Malala was given a standing ovation by the 1,000-strong audience as she was awarded an honorary masters degree from

Edinburgh University. She said: "Thank you so much for giving me this opportunity to talk to you today. I'm here for the first time and it's really nice to see Scotland. I'm enjoying the hills, small hills, because we have mountains in Pakistan. After I was shot the terrorists thought that I would not continue the struggle for education, but not only did I not stop my campaign but now Kainat and Shazia are with me and they are also supporting me. They are not afraid, we are not afraid and now people are supporting us and that is the greatest courage, and that is the weapon that we have got, the unity and togetherness. For achieving my goal, people must be united, they must work together and that is why I feel empowered."

She added that she hoped to get straight As in her GCSEs, which she was studying for at school in Birmingham, and to go on to university. Gordon Brown, who was a UN envoy for global education, said Malala was a symbol of courage, bravery and resilience around the world, and represented "someone prepared to make a huge sacrifice for a cause". He said: "She has proved to us that neither threats, intimidation or violence will ever silence her voice to speak up for what she believes, and what I believe, is one of the great civil rights struggles of our time. I'm so pleased to see her reunited with Shazia and Kainat, two young women equally determined that every girl and boy should enjoy the most basic of human rights: a secure, safe place at school."

That same month, Taliban commander Qari Nasrullah, with his head wrapped in an Afghan scarf, left only his eyes uncovered to avoid the many spy agencies hunting him when he gave a face-to-face interview with a *Daily Mirror* reporter. The reporter said: "In his Pashto tongue of the lawless tribal border between Pakistan's north west frontier and Afghanistan, he told me chillingly: 'I am told you can be trusted, but I warn you I must ask you not to break that trust and identify my face. I trust you when you say there will be no secret filming.' What followed was an invaluable insight into the twisted logic of an enemy mind." Equally disturbing was the fact that this terror veteran was adamant the Taliban will once again rule Afghanistan with an iron fist and return to the dark days of strict Sharia rule once NATO troops leave. "I pressed the slim rebel about the terrible toll his comrades have inflicted on NATO troops since the US-led invasion of 2001. A total of 3,274 coalition soldiers have died, including 444 Brits, 2,161 Americans and thousands of others left crippled and maimed in the war, sparked by the suicide attacks on the Twin Towers in New York.

"With a blank stare, he replied coldly: 'Regarding your soldiers' death toll, when they travel that far to fight a war they are definitely not going to be presented with flowers and there will be deaths for sure. Thousands of our men have been martyred and as for your soldiers, we did not go after them to other countries. They came to our country and they have been torturing us and have sabotaged our government.' Showing not a shred of remorse over the deaths, he added with a dismissive wave of the hand: 'Anyway, this is what happens in war.' Nasrullah also told how the Taliban vowed to again run Afghanistan after NATO leaves in 2015.

"Worryingly for this battered country, I knew this meant a return to barbarity that includes public executions for infidelity, beheadings and punishment beatings for disobeying a twisted version of the Islamic law. Nasrullah, who along with thousands of other Taliban had waged war against British and other NATO forces for more than a decade, said: 'In Afghanistan, praise be to God, we are heading towards success. We are approaching total success as most of the country is now under our control.'" The reporter ended the secret meeting with the words, "we were only too aware of the dangers posed by this man and his cohorts".

The interview provided a "remarkable glimpse into the mind of the enemy" the newspaper claimed. Other journalists had nothing but the utmost respect for the *Daily Mirror*'s Chris Hughes and Andrew Stenning, who had faced the Taliban terror chief. They went to meet Qari Nasrullah only too aware of the brutal beheading of American journalist Daniel Pearl in Pakistan in 2002 at the hands of Nasrullah's brother in jihad, the 9/11 planner Khalid Shaykh Mohammed. Their huge risk was rewarded with a remarkable and significant interview. "As well as a conspirator to mass murder, Nasrullah, like so many Taliban leaders, is a deluded and confused liar", said another article published that same day. "He lies when he says that the only civilians his people harm are those near NATO bases." The truth was that up to the beginning of October 2013, over 300 civilians had died following deliberate Taliban targeting. Several of these had been murdered in Kunar province, undoubtedly on the orders of the *shura* of which Nasrullah is a member. As of that point in the year, 86 per cent of all civilian deaths had been caused directly, or indirectly, by the Taliban. The article continued: "Nasrullah lies too about education under the Taliban, claiming they allowed girls' schools. He has conveniently forgotten his leader's edict that no girls were to be educated beyond the age of eight. Under Western protection 4 million girls are in education for the first time in Afghanistan." But Nasrullah and his men had been intent on turning the clocks back by bombing, burning or intimidating hundreds of girls' schools into closure. Nasrullah complained that the West entered Afghanistan unprovoked, ignoring the reality that US and British intervention followed a refusal by Taliban leader Mullah Omar to hand over those responsible for the 9/11 attacks that killed 3,000 people. It is tragically inevitable that after NATO withdrawal, many Afghans will again be forced to live under the Taliban's mediaeval reign of terror, especially in the south and east. The report stated: "Those that believe the Afghan Taliban have no violent ambitions outside the country should note both Nasrullah's continuing reverence for Osama Bin Laden, the icon of international terrorists, and his threat that there is 'no boundary for jihad'." Hotels, schools, aid workers and marketplaces are "legitimate" targets for the Taliban.

A serious war crime committed by the Taliban has been the placing of bombs along transit routes, which has contributed to at least three quarters of all civilian deaths for which they are responsible. However, the United States has also had a part to play in the number of deaths during the Afghan conflict. In Asadabad in Kunar province, Abdul Wali, a prisoner at a US base, was killed by David Passaro. He was convicted on one count of felony assault with a dangerous weapon. Two years later, in 2005, a US army report revealed that US armed forces were responsible for the deaths of two civilian Afghan prisoners in 2002 in Bagram. The two unarmed men were chained to the ceiling and beaten to death. Military coroners ruled homicide in both cases. Seven soldiers were charged, and in 2010 five more were charged with murder for killing three Afghan civilians in Kandahar and collecting body parts as trophies. Then, in 2012, in what became known as the Kandahar massacre, 16 civilians, 11 of whom came from the same family, nine of whom were just children, were brutally murdered by US army Staff Sergeant Robert Bales. He was charged with 16 counts of premeditated murder and the wounding of six others.

The Libyan Civil War

2011

On the weekend of 20th March 2011, a *Daily Mirror* reporter wrote: "On this very weekend in 2003 I was sleeping in my tent on Kuwait's border with Iraq when I was awoken by helicopters and fighter jets screaming overhead. The war on Iraq had begun. Eight years on and, make no mistake, we are at war again. And once more it is with a despot who has brutalised his own people." The build-up to Iraq was long and drawn-out; the decision to attack Colonel Gaddafi was as sudden as it was surprising. But even if the conflict with Libya was designed to be much more limited and focused, the problems remained the same. The journalist continued: "It is easy to commit to military action. It is far, far harder to end it. And very rarely does it end in the way you imagine. David Cameron deserves credit for leading the charge at the UN, which for once has acted with speed and decisiveness. But for the Prime Minister it is a pivotal moment. A high-risk move that could define his premiership. This is Cameron's war and this time it's Britain dragging along a reluctant America."

The moral case for stopping Gaddafi's military in its tracks was difficult to argue against. The priority was to prevent more slaughter in Benghazi, or anywhere else, and there was a good chance it would work. The UN resolution allowed international forces to go much further than simply enforcing a no-fly zone. It allowed attacks on Gaddafi's tanks, artillery and ground troops should they threaten civilians in any way. Britain, France and America had the ability to launch precise and deadly air strikes, which it was hoped would keep Gaddafi quiet for some time. However, there was a problem. What if the wily Libyan leader decided to do nothing and simply kept his troops where they were? If he abided by the ceasefire, then what could Britain and the others do? The journalist said: "It could turn into a long, costly stalemate with British pilots flying endless missions over a Libya split in half but with Gaddafi still in control." The real question was whether the resolution allowed international forces to attack the regime itself. Could they attack Gaddafi's compounds and try to kill him and his sons? How easy would that be without troops on the ground? Maybe it could be justified under the banner of "all measures necessary to protect civilians". This was, however, the beginning of the end. What was really exercising minds at the White House at this point was the possibility of Bahrain's uprising spreading to Saudi Arabia.

On 9th April 2011 a Red Cross ship carrying vital medical supplies docked in the besieged Libyan town of Misrata just as aid workers entered the battleground town of Zawiyah. These humanitarian breakthroughs brought some relief for residents of the rebel-held cities, who had been left desperate after six weeks of fighting. British jets had destroyed seven tanks belonging to forces loyal to Colonel Muammar Gaddafi, seen making defiant gestures on TV on the same day as rebels pushed towards Brega oil port. Another 17 tanks were destroyed by other NATO planes. But 30 rebels were killed by Gaddafi soldiers in an attack in Misrata. The world held its breath towards the end of August 2011 when Gaddafi was reported to be on the run after rebels overran his Tripoli base. He was believed to have been in hiding in a bunker underneath the city since the air strikes began. By 24th August, SAS fighters dressed in Arab civilian clothing were said to be flushing out tunnels beneath Tripoli in the hunt for the dictator. These rumours hit the headlines day after day, indicating that he had fled Tripoli and was headed for Sabha after fleeing from a farm based outside his former city. The farm was captured by rebels, but Gaddafi was nowhere to be seen. By 7th September, it was cited that he had been seen heading for Libya's southern borders with Chad or Niger. However, on 20th October 2011, after the dictator's son Mutassim was captured trying to escape from Sirte, Gaddafi was found and killed.

Less than a month later, begging for mercy and pleading not to be shot, Colonel Gaddafi's once-defiant son was finally captured... The fingers of his right hand wrapped tightly in bandages, fugitive Saif al-Islam Gaddafi later cut a humbled and dejected figure as he cowered on a prison bed after a month on the run. The playboy prince – wanted for crimes against humanity – was ambushed... by Libyan troops who traced him to the desert at Obari, 400 miles south of the capital Tripoli. He tried to flee but his car got stuck, forcing him to give himself up. Then he begged them not to shoot him. Saif was the last key member of former Libyan leader Colonel Gaddafi's family to be captured or killed.

His arrest followed a night of fierce clashes between militiamen and Gaddafi loyalists in an oasis town near the Niger border. Ahmed al-Zintani, one of Saif's captors, said his unit of 15 men in three vehicles, acting on intelligence reports, stopped two cars carrying Gaddafi and four others. Gaddafi was in the second vehicle. Saif, Gaddafi's oldest son, pretended he was somebody else, but the fighters quickly recognized him. Terrified of meeting the same fate as his dead father and brother Mutassim, he begged: "Please don't shoot me, please don't shoot me!" Mr al-Zintani said: "At the beginning he was very scared. He thought we would kill him. When the first car came forward we surrounded them and they didn't resist. Then the second car came up. They tried to escape and they got stuck in the sand. Saif came out with three others."

It was a low-key end in contrast to Saif's bravado over that summer when he appeared on TV to boast that he remained free, and had claimed: "We have broken the backbone of the rebels." The captive, once heir-apparent to his father, was flown to an army base in the town of Zintan, 85 miles southwest of Tripoli. During the flight he insisted to journalists that he was "feeling fine" – but the pictures of him told a different story. Some reports said he was suffering from anaemia and malnutrition after a month living as a fugitive. A mob tried to storm the plane as it landed. The crowd was held back by police for an hour before he could be brought off the plane. His capture was greeted with celebrations and gunfire across Libya. He had reportedly been trying to flee to Niger, where he was expected to be offered asylum, despite being indicted by the International Criminal Court for the bombing and shooting of protesters in February 2011. He was last seen on 20th October – the day his father was killed in Sirte. Libya's ruling National Transitional Council insisted it would try war criminals in Libya and not extradite them to the International Criminal Court. But they faced huge pressure to send him to The Hague for trial. Gaddafi faced the death penalty if tried in Libya. Prime Minister David Cameron said of his capture: "It is a great achievement for the Libyan people and must now become a victory for international justice too." Libya's Prime Minister designate Abdurrahim El-Keib said: "We assure Libyans and the world that Saif al-Islam will receive a fair trial... under fair legal processes which our own people had been deprived of for the last 40 years."

The Syrian Civil War

2011–

Veteran war journalist Marie Colvin was killed on 22nd February 2012 in Syria, hours after reporting on "sickening scenes" in war-torn Homs. Colvin was killed by Syrian forces while covering the bloody siege of the city of Homs for a British newspaper. Her death, along with that of French photographer Ochlik, 28, came just hours after she had reported on events in the stricken city and slammed regime "lies". Witnesses said the American-born journalist was fired on by a rocket as she and Mr Ochlik fled a makeshift media centre that had been shelled in a heavy artillery barrage by Syrian forces. As the centre – which was situated next to a hospital – began to collapse, journalists and guides fled the scene in the Baba Amr district and were fired upon again by Syrian soldiers. Colvin, who was in her 50s, appeared on Channel 4 and ITN's *News at Ten* on the Tuesday evening just prior to her death, reporting on the bombardment of the opposition stronghold. In a piece for the *Sunday Times* at the weekend, Colvin spoke of the citizens of the city "waiting for a massacre". She wrote: "The scale of human tragedy in the city is immense. The inhabitants are living in terror. Almost every family seems to have suffered the death or injury of a loved one." In a TV report for American viewers, Colvin branded Syrian regime claims that troops were fighting terrorists and not attacking civilians as "lies".

It was feared that journalists were being deliberately targeted in Syria after a French TV cameraman was killed the previous month by mortar shells. Throughout her career Colvin covered many conflicts around the globe, including Tunisia, Egypt and Libya during the Arab Spring. In 2010, at a Fleet Street memorial for Western journalists killed in conflicts, Colvin spoke about the dangers of reporting on war zones. The reporter – who famously wore an eye-patch after losing an eye in a rocket attack in Sri Lanka in 2001 – told an audience at St Brides Church in Fleet Street: "Craters. Burned houses. Mutilated bodies. Women weeping for children and husbands. Men for their wives, mothers, children. Our mission is to report these horrors of war with accuracy and without prejudice. We always have to ask ourselves whether the level of risk is worth the story. What is bravery, and what is bravado? Journalists covering combat shoulder great responsibilities and face difficult choices. Sometimes they pay the ultimate price."

Colvin worked in Chechnya, Kosovo, Sierra Leone and Sri Lanka, in the latter of which she was injured and lost her eye in an ambush when she was targeted by government soldiers because of her work with the Tamil Tigers. She won the British press award for "Best Foreign Correspondent" twice for her work reporting on conflicts in Yugoslavia, Iran, Sri Lanka and Zimbabwe. She also won the International Women's Media Foundation award for "Courage in Journalism" for her coverage of Kosovo and

Chechnya, along with the Foreign Press Association's Journalist of the Year award. Colvin wrote and produced the BBC documentary *Arafat: Behind the Myth* and presented another documentary on Martha Gellhorn, the war correspondent famed for her coverage of the Spanish Civil War. Earlier in 2012, photographer Ochlik won a World Press Photo Award for his work in Libya in 2011.

It was also reported that Rami al-Sayed, a citizen journalist who provided media outlets with live footage from Homs, was killed in the shelling, while British photojournalist Paul Conroy, who had worked closely with Ms Colvin in the past, was also injured. That day as many as 60 died in Homs after the city came under heavy shelling. Activists warned of a new round of fierce and bloody urban combat being unleashed, despite efforts by the Red Cross to broker a ceasefire to allow emergency aid in. Shells reportedly rained down in the previous few days on rebellious districts at a rate of 10 per minute at one point, and the Red Cross called for a daily two-hour ceasefire so that it could deliver emergency aid to the wounded and sick. It was also reported that food and water were running dangerously low in the city.

Marie Colvin's 30-year career in journalism saw her take up the post of Paris bureau chief for United Press International in 1984 before she moved to the *Sunday Times* a year later. There, she was Middle East correspondent from 1986 to 1995 before becoming foreign affairs correspondent. Colvin's role was pivotal in bringing the world news from inside war-torn borders.

Had she lived, she would no doubt have reported on the

terrible chemical attacks that took place in Syria in August 2013. On the 22nd of that month, the world awoke to horrifying pictures of innocent children lying dead. Many of the victims were found huddled in their beds as if still sleeping. Others died in agony, convulsing and foaming at the mouth. They were among more than 1,000 Syrian civilians, including men, women and children, who were massacred in a suspected chemical-weapons attack. The slaughter – the worst atrocity of the nation's brutal civil war – came just days after a United Nations weapons-inspection team arrived in Syria. Responsibility for the sarin-style nerve-gas bombardment in the Al Ghouta area, east of the capital Damascus, was immediately denied by President Bashar al-Assad's beleaguered regime. Officials dismissed the claims as "illogical and fabricated". They said it was a sign of "hysteria and floundering" by the government's enemies. But, as shocking pictures of the carnage were beamed around the world, there were mounting calls for military intervention. Foreign Secretary William Hague vowed that the culprits would be held to account. He added: "If verified, this would mark a shocking escalation in the use of chemical weapons in Syria."

His concern was echoed by the European Union, which stressed the need for a "thorough and immediate" investigation. The Turkish Foreign Ministry branded the killings "a crime against humanity". Unverified images included lines of apparently dead children, their bodies wrapped in shrouds ready for burial. The death toll was said to be the highest for a single day in the two and a half years of civil war up to that point, which had claimed more than 100,000 lives on all sides. Rebels claimed Assad's troops launched a desperate artillery bombardment against pockets of resistance outside east Damascus early on 21st August 2013. The Britain-based Syrian Observatory for Human Rights, which relies on contacts within Syria, said the shelling was intense and that it hit the eastern suburbs of Zamalka, Arbeen and Ein Tarma. They claimed the military fired "rockets with poisonous gas heads" in the 3.00 am attack. Rescuer Abu Nidal told of the chilling scenes following the shelling. He said: "We would go into a house and everything was in its place, every person was in their place. They were lying where they had been. They looked like they were asleep. But they were dead, entire families. We saw men collapsed on staircases and in doorways. It looked like they were trying to go in and help and were then overcome themselves."

Survivor Farah al-Shami, from the town of Mouadamiya, southwest of the capital, said she thought her region was too close to a military encampment to be affected. She said: "At the same time the UN was here – it seemed impossible. But then I started to feel dizzy. I was choking and my eyes were burning." Majid Abu Ali, a doctor in the eastern suburb of Douma, said in a Skype interview: "The injuries correspond with sarin gas – difficulty breathing, perspiration, convulsions and loss of consciousness to the point of death." Another doctor, Abu Omar, said he was swamped with casualties, including nine rescuers who had also died. He added: "We didn't know what to do there were so many cases. At first they were being affected by the gas. But now they're dying in the regular shelling. The bombs just won't stop."

President Barack Obama had warned earlier in the year that the use of chemical weapons would mean crossing a "clear red line". In May 2013, the *Daily Mirror* exclusively revealed that British spies had obtained proof of chemical weapons being used in Syria. Samples sent to the MoD's research labs in Porton Down, Wiltshire, tested positive. Russia's foreign ministry, which had backed Assad and vetoed UN attempts to intervene, called for a "fair and professional investigation" into the latest slaughter. The deputy head of the Western-backed Syria National Coalition, George Sabra, claimed in Istanbul that 1,300 people had died. He said: "Today's crimes are not the first time the regime has used chemical weapons. But they constitute a significant turning point... this time it was for annihilation rather than terror." The UN backed a call by Secretary General Ban Ki-moon for a "thorough, impartial and prompt investigation" into the alleged attack. Only Russia and China, allies of Assad's regime, quibbled over the wording of the call. Some observers claimed the severity of the attack just three days after UN inspectors arrived made it "unlikely" the regime was guilty. Rolf Ekeus, a former UN weapons inspector in Iraq, said: "It would be very peculiar if they were to do this at the exact moment the international inspectors come into the country."

By 6th October 2013, Western intelligence estimated that

President al-Assad could have had more than 1,000 tons of nerve agents and poison gases. However, around this time experts had begun destroying Syria's chemical weapons. Monitoring officials told the BBC that the Organisation for the Prohibition of Chemical Weapons (OPCW) had begun dismantling the country's stockpile as part of a UN resolution and agreement drawn up by Russia and the US. America and other Western powers said the attack was carried out by President Bashar al-Assad's forces, but he repeatedly denied this. Syria was then ordered to destroy all its chemical weapons equipment by the end of August 2013, and its stockpile of poison gas by the following year. These conditions were part of the deal thrashed out by the US and Russia, who said that Assad could avoid American military action if he abandoned his chemical arsenal and allowed weapons experts unfettered access.

The Home Secretary, Theresa May, said in following news reports that she was aware that British residents had gone to Somalia and Syria for training and to fight. Syria, it seemed, was becoming a training ground for potential UK terrorists, she warned. If they returned to the UK they could pose a potential "terrorist" threat, she said. "What we have seen for some time now is certainly people here in the UK travelling out, a limited number of people, people travelling out to Somalia, we're now seeing people travelling out to Syria. Some of those are potential terrorists who will get training, in some cases actually engage in conflict and then potentially return to the UK."

The Home Secretary had secretly stripped British citizenship from members of an alleged London cell linked to the al-Shabaab terrorist group. At least four men with links to the organization behind the Kenyan shopping-centre massacre had had their passports removed on security grounds. Ms May refused to rule out that British shopping centres could be vulnerable to similar attacks, but indicated that the possibility was high on the agenda of the police and security services.

The Home Secretary was also planning to put immigration enforcement officers in every main police station as part of a crackdown on foreign criminals. The Home Office estimated that there are some 5,500 organized crime groups in the UK, with a quarter of them made up of overseas nationals. Labour's Home Affairs spokesman Chris Bryant MP said: "Theresa May is still failing on immigration and this Bill is not going to address some of the biggest problems. The number of foreign criminals deported has dropped by over 13 per cent since the election, border checks have been cut with only half as many people stopped and illegal immigration has got worse."

There was a slight lift in news with regard to Syria when it was reported on 11th October 2013 that the OPCW had been rewarded "for extensive efforts to eliminate chemical weapons". The global weapons inspection watchdog responsible for trying to destroy Syria's nerve-gas stockpiles had won a Nobel Peace Prize. The Norwegian Nobel Committee handed the award to the OPCW "for its extensive efforts to eliminate chemical weapons".

A committee spokesman added: "The conventions and the work of the OPCW have defined the use of chemical weapons as a taboo under international law. Recent events in Syria, where chemical weapons have again been put to use, have underlined the need to enhance the efforts to do away with such weapons." However, in a tweet the committee stressed that the OPCW had not been given the peace prize for its work in Syria. The OPCW was founded in 1997 to implement the Chemical Weapons Convention signed on January 13, 1993, and was supervising the dismantling of Syria's chemical arsenal and facilities under the terms of a UN Security Council resolution.

Just two days later, the news took a "dive" once again when it was announced on 13th October that the Red Cross humanitarian agency had appealed for the release of six Red Cross workers and a local volunteer in northwest Syria, who had been abducted by gunmen. Reports from Syria suggested that the gunmen opened fire on the vehicles carrying the aid workers before seizing them and taking them to an unknown location. The International Committee of the Red Cross (ICRC) appealed for the seven workers to be freed immediately. Spokesman Ewan Watson, who declined to reveal the nationalities or gender of the six ICRC staff, said: "I am able to confirm that six ICRC staff members and one Syrian Arab Red Crescent volunteer have been abducted near Idlib in northwestern Syria. We are calling for the immediate and unconditional release of this team which was delivering humanitarian assistance to those most in need – and we do that on both sides of the front lines." Watson also said the team's vehicles were missing. The team had been on their way back to Damascus after delivering medical supplies in Sarmin and Idlib. Syrian state media reported the incident earlier in the day, saying the gunmen had kidnapped the Red Cross workers after opening fire on their vehicles. Quoting an unnamed official, state news agency SANA said the workers were travelling in the Idlib area when gunmen blocked their path, shot at their convoy, seized them and took them to an unknown location.

"An armed terrorist group today kidnapped a number of workers in the mission of the International Committee of the Red Cross in Syria" the report said, using a term the government frequently uses for rebels trying to topple President Bashar al-Assad. Kidnappings had become increasingly common in northern Syria, where rebels had captured swathes of territory but government forces clung on to many urban centres, and fighting continued daily. By this time, the two-and-a-half-year conflict had claimed more than 100,000 lives and driven more than 2.1 million refugees out of their shattered homeland.

On 19th October, vascular surgeon David Nott said he saw two heavily pregnant women being treated for gunshot wounds, with their babies dead in the womb. Syrian snipers were targeting pregnant rebel women in the Syrian war, the British surgeon on the front line revealed. Nott, a surgeon based at London's Chelsea and Westminster Hospital, who had also volunteered in Bosnia and Libya, said: "The women were all shot through the uterus, so that must have been where they were aiming for. This is the first time I have seen anything like this. This was beyond deliberate. It was hell beyond hell." Syria Relief was among three charities that supported Nott's trip. It issued an X-ray of a full-term foetus with a bullet in its skull.

On 23rd October, terrified shipwreck victims were left 100 miles off the Maltese coast after Libyan traffickers sank their boat over a pay dispute. Men, women and children were discovered 160 km off the coast of Malta, after their fishing boat was reportedly shot and sunk by traffickers in a row over payment. The shocking footage that accompanied news reports showed the moment the survivors were found and rescued by the Maltese Navy in October 2013. According to reports from Al Jazeera news, around 400 refugees were on board the rickety fishing boat, which had left the Libyan coast on 10th October. It was estimated that 200 people perished when the boat went down, plunging those on board into the deep water. Some were wearing lifejackets to help them stay afloat while others swam for their lives, with no hope of ever reaching the shore. A lucky few made it into lifeboats while others were plucked from the water by survivors. The video of the scenes came as the European Union government heads met in Brussels to discuss a proposal put forward by Malta. The country had raised concerns about the waters in the area, which had been the site of several shipwrecks in recent months.

The activities of traffickers were back in the news on 27th October when it emerged that a criminal gang's activities were raising serious concerns that terrorist organizations such as al-Qaeda could use similar tactics to sneak jihadists into Europe. The people-trafficking gang was raking in millions of pounds by bringing hundreds of Syrian refugees into the UK. The gang in Istanbul, Turkey, told undercover investigators that for £34,000 they would smuggle three men to the UK from Syria using minders and false passports. The investigators had earlier met a Syrian woman who used her life savings to pay the gang to help her flee after being tortured in her home country. The teacher, who they called Ishtar to protect her identity, was then living in southern England. She told how traffickers got her from Turkey to Britain after handing her a false passport. The gang's activities raised serious concerns that terrorist organizations such as al-Qaeda could use similar tactics to sneak jihadists into all parts of Europe. The investigators were alerted to the criminal organization by an anonymous phone call to their London offices. One investigator was warned: "This trade is making millions for Turkish gangs. They have fixers around Europe and in the UK flying people across Europe. They have people working in airports who look the other way. They are taking Syrians to Italy, Holland and the Scandinavian countries, but Britain is the most expensive. On landing, the Syrian asks for asylum. They are often out of the airport within three hours because nobody is going to send them back to a country where people are being killed by chemical weapons." Ishtar told the investigators how she escaped and why she turned to the traffickers. She said: "Hundreds of Syrians pay gangs in Turkey to get them into Britain so they can apply for asylum. I used my life savings and my family's gold to pay a gang €13,000 (£11,000) to help me start a new life in safety. The gang took my picture and for 10 days I waited with hundreds of terrified Syrian refugees in an Istanbul hotel. Eventually the call telling me it was time to leave came. I was introduced to a gang member called 'Nasar' and told not to ask questions. 'They told me "you are not allowed to speak to him"'."

She was driven to Istanbul airport with the minder. She said: "The gang got me past security with my passport and a ticket to Lebanon, which we are allowed to go to. It was made to look like I was flying to Beirut but I followed my guide and boarded a plane to Vienna with a false passport he gave me." From Austria they flew to Oslo before she was driven to Sweden for a British Airways flight to London. Ishtar said: "We travelled for a day and a half. I never spoke to him. He passed me the passport only when I needed it and then took it back. I did not know if we would be caught or captured and I was shaking at the thought of being taken back to Syria. When we arrived at Heathrow he took the passport off me and I walked up to the immigration desk and said I wanted to apply for asylum."

In another story, gang boss Abu Nasar boasted to a newspaper investigator how easy it was to get a Syrian refugee on a flight for Heathrow with a forged passport. He said: "Get me pictures and photographs for them [for their new passport] and it won't be a problem." Revealing how his gang preyed on refugees with nowhere else to turn, he said: "You deposit the money in an office. We get the money once he is on the flight." Sitting outside a coffee shop near a bustling Istanbul plaza, Nasar told the reporter he did not care where people came from, he only cared about the money. He said: "This work I don't do unless I am certain there will be no trouble. It's not in my interest to have him arrested." Asked if he had people turning a blind eye to his forged passports in airport departure terminals, Nasar smiled and said: "Going towards Britain? Yes." The informant said: "Syrians and other Middle Eastern refugees have no choice but to use gangs to acquire convincing paperwork to fly into Europe. There are no embassies left in Syria to get visas. After paying a set fee to a middle man who acts as a guarantor – or *kafeel* in Arabic – for the money, they await further instructions at a safe house or hotel in Istanbul. The guarantor is normally a highly respected businessman who gives you a password which you only tell the gang once you safely arrive in Britain. The client is told to await a call from the gang. When it comes they follow their man straight away. He hands them a false passport when they need it."

The previous week it was reported that there were more than 600,000 Syrians in Turkey, 400,000 of them in refugee camps. Turkey, Jordan and Iraq had taken in 2.2 million fleeing refugees, and 2 million more were expected the following year. The investigation discovered scores of desperate Syrians who had paid the gangs and were waiting for the signal. One night, they contacted gang boss Nasar from a Turkish phone number.

He said: "If you want to go through details for one or two hours we can meet tomorrow. But if it is a quick meeting we can do that in a bit. I will send somebody to pick you up." The reporter was collected by Nasar's deputy Kosai, who walked the reporter to the meeting. On the way, Kosai told four Syrian refugees waiting for Nasar's call: "You will only know one hour ahead." Nasar greeted the investigators with a handshake and asked: "Where do you want to go and what's the destination?" After being told the drop-off point, Nasar smiled: "It's not a problem but it's expensive." The reporter said he wanted to smuggle his elderly dad and two brothers into the UK. Nasar said: "No way three of them could go together. Maybe the youngsters go first, maybe your dad. What way do you want them to go to England? Through Greece? If you want to take them from there you can. If you want us to do it we will. If you have his passport copy ready I'll tell you when."

Nasar then took an urgent call from someone else and told them it would cost €1,000 (£850) each to handle 10 people. Turning his attention back to the reporter, he added: "Initially, as I said to you, it will be €16,000. There are two ways. One is to pay €16,000 and if anything happens there is a different way and that is €14,000." He said he had "loads" of people who could transfer cash for him in Istanbul. Asked what would happen if the client got caught, he said: "No, no, no… there's no trouble.

"They [the Turkish Border Police] will stop him for five hours then they will be released. Syrians are the first ones to

War Crimes

get released." The next day the reporter met guarantor Cemal Seyhsait at his office. Kosai said that Seyhsait, in his 50s, was trustworthy. Accompanied by guards, Seyhsait said personal codes he gave customers protected their money transfers. He said: "Your money will go into my account and I give you a receipt and a code. When you get to the destination you ring me and tell me to pay Abu Nasar or give the code to him and once he tells me the code I pay him. I wouldn't give you the money back without agreeing with Abu Nasar." He said he charged a 0.5 per cent fee on cash he transferred, and that the reporter should pay £34,055 for three men to fly to Britain. Calling a money arranger in the UK to introduce him to the reporter, he set up a call to hand over the money. He said: "When you have the money, give me the OK." The guarantor waved the reporter goodbye, adding: "If relatives or friends want to do business, this is my card." The National Crime Agency said it would study the investigator's dossier.

The horrific ordeal that Syrian President Assad's brutal forces put terrified Ishtar through convinced her that she had to flee her homeland. Breaking down in tears she said: "I had to leave Syria after being arrested, tortured and raped by the Syrian intelligence forces." Ishtar bravely spoke out about the illicit trafficking trade and the terrible treatment of ordinary Syrians, especially women. She sobbed: "I was shaking and scared but I knew I had to take the risk and flee.

"In April Assad's people took me from my home in Damascus

when my brother refused to join the army. For 10 days they hanged me by my arms with chains and tortured me. Then they raped me. After they let me go they dumped me in the middle of nowhere and it took my family three days to find me. My family and I escaped to Egypt before I flew on my own to Istanbul to meet a family member who helped organise for me to be smuggled to the UK."

On 27th October frustrated relatives of Britons claimed officials were dragging their feet over visa applications from their family members and spouses. The government was accused of "actively leaving" the relatives of British nationals in danger in Syria by delaying the processing of visa applications. Campaigners and relatives then urged officials to prioritize visa applications from the spouses and family members who were trapped in the war-torn country. A petition launched on campaign website Avaaz called on them to recognize the "exceptional circumstances" they face, and to allow them to join their relatives and partners in the UK. The petition had gathered more than 700 signatures by this point, but families wanted more people to back their campaign to force the government to take action. Christine Gilmore said her husband Ziad was stuck in Damascus in "absolutely dire" circumstances, and accused officials of actively leaving him in danger. Ms Gilmore, 33, met her 50-year-old husband in Damascus, where she spent a year as part of a masters degree studying Arabic. After meeting in May 2010 the couple decide to marry, and they underwent a marriage ceremony in Syria in October 2011. But she claimed that their attempts to get him a visa so he could join her in the UK and escape the dangers of Syria had failed, despite meeting income and English language requirements.

They were waiting for the results of his latest application, but Ms Gilmore accused the government of "trying to find every excuse" to prevent her husband from coming to the UK. "I naively thought that if you are a British citizen and you have your husband or wife or parents or children in a war zone that they would do something to expedite them being able to come and join you. But it seems they are actually doing the complete opposite." She claimed to know at least a dozen British people in a similar situation, whose visa applications for Syrian spouses or relatives had all been refused. "How can they get away with that?" she said. "What surprises me is that they ought to be facilitating that, this is an emergency." She called for more discretion by officials when looking at cases, especially taking into account the difficulties in getting all the necessary documents in a country where the infrastructure is failing due to on-going violence, and problems getting to specific English language test centres. "They are not taking any of that on board and they have the power to do so if they wanted to. It just seems scandalous. I can understand that they might not want to take a quota of refugees like some countries, but to actively leave your family members in great danger is so cynical, it's beyond belief.

"The situation out there is absolutely dire, there's no electricity in the whole of southern Syria, there's attacks constantly, he nearly got killed by a car bomb, he has been shot at. It destroys your life knowing the person you love is there." She said she started the petition out of "incredible frustration" over the situation, adding: "It's far from being just a Syrian issue, it's very widespread."

Shafik Salih, 42, of east London, said he was suffering in the same situation, as an application for his Syrian fiancée Nesrin, 33, had been refused. The couple, who met when Mr Salih was visiting Damascus in 2008, got engaged in December 2012, but a visa application for Nesrin was refused early in 2013. They were awaiting an appeal, due to be heard in April 2014. Mr Salih said: "I talk to my fiancée every day on Skype, chat and phone. The electricity is available for short periods, the internet connection is very bad.

"My fiancée is ill and she needs medications. The security position is very dangerous up there and I am worried about her. My fiancée is in a war zone in Syria. She is in real danger and needs urgent health care." He said he was not convinced by the reasons given for refusing a visa, which he said included the alleged failure to provide correct documentation, and insisted he and his fiancée met all the requirements for her to come to the UK.

"I think I do not need to explain about her dangerous situation in Syria and my devastating situation here in the UK" he said. "It is a basic human right to allow reunion of the family members. In our case, the issue is not just a human rights issue, but it is a life issue." A Home Office spokeswoman said: "All visa applications are considered on their individual merits and in line with the immigration rules. We have put special arrangements in place for a visa concession, which will allow Syrians already lawfully in the country to extend their permission to stay in the UK without returning home, where appropriate."

On 31st October President Bashar al-Assad's regime met the deadline set by the OPCW. It was reported that Syria had destroyed all of its chemical weapons production facilities following the suspected sarin attack that killed hundreds of its own people.

Documents revealed that the watchdog's teams had inspected 21 out of 23 deadly sites across Syria – the remaining two were too dangerous to examine. However, the chemical equipment had already been moved to other sites experts visited, proving that the deadly substances had been destroyed. Papers on the destruction of chemical weapon sites in Syria said: "The OPCW is satisfied it has verified, and seen destroyed, all declared critical production/mixing/filling equipment from all 23 sites."

Under the disarmament timetable, Syria was due to render all chemical production and weapons-filling facilities unusable by 1st November 2013 – a target that it met. By the middle of 2014, it was ordered that Syria should have destroyed its entire stockpile of chemical weapons. As of late 2013, about 120,000 people were thought to have been killed in more than two years of bitter fighting in the civil war. It was believed that more than 100 British jihadist fighters could have travelled to Syria to take up arms alongside rebel factions who are trying to oust Assad.

Another worry with regard to the civil war was the threat of a re-emergence of outbreaks of disease, including polio. Reporting on 8th November 2013, the *Daily Mirror* said that Europe was declared free of the disease in 2002 but that a recent outbreak in Syria had created concern for countries with low immunization rates. Doctors warned that refugees fleeing war-torn Syria could bring polio back to Europe. Two German infection specialists said that the vaccine used in parts of the EU was not 100 per cent effective and feared that low immunization levels in Bosnia, Ukraine and Austria could trigger an outbreak. At this time, the World Health Organization (WHO) confirmed an outbreak of at least 10 cases of polio in Syria, where vaccination coverage had dramatically decreased because of the civil war. With large numbers of people fleeing Syria and seeking refuge in neighbouring countries and Europe, experts feared that the disease could reappear in areas that had been free of it for decades. Professor Martin Eichner and Dr Stefan Brockmann said in *The Lancet*: "Vaccinating only refugees must be judged as insufficient. More comprehensive measures should be taken into consideration." The polio vaccine used in most European countries was the inactivated polio vaccine (IPC), which was injected. It usually formed part of a combined diphtheria, tetanus, whooping cough and polio jab. While good at preventing paralysis, the IPC provides only partial protection from infection,

Prof Eichner and Dr Brockmann pointed out. "Once children were routinely vaccinated with an oral polio vaccine (OPV), taken in the form of mouth drops, which uses a live virus and is more effective. But this was discontinued in the UK and many other countries because in rare cases it can trigger paralysis."

In late November 2013, there were unconfirmed reports that Mohammed el-Araj, a Muslim in his 20s, was the second Briton to die fighting in the war-torn country of Syria. Araj, from Ladbroke Grove, west London, was killed in mid-August 2013, according to newspaper reports. His family was reported to have told reporters that he grew up in the UK after being born on a British Airways flight. Araj was believed to have been associated with jihadist organizations including Jabhat al-Nusra, a militant group linked to al-Qaeda. Shiraz Maher, of the International Centre for the Study of Radicalistion (ICSR), said he was believed to have been fighting in and around Idlib province in the north of the country. Araj was arrested in 2009 and jailed for 18 months following violent protests outside the Israeli Embassy in London, according to some newspapers. In May another Briton, 22-year-old Londoner Ali al Manasfi, was reported killed while fighting in Syria. It was stated that he died while photographing military positions near the Turkish border.

News reports stated on 25th November that, in a major breakthrough, the opposition Syrian National Coalition had agreed to take part in a peace conference in Switzerland called "Geneva II". Hopes for a peace deal in Syria then rose after the warring sides agreed to a new round of talks early in 2014. The United Nations said there would be "a peace conference in Geneva, Switzerland, on January 22" aimed at ending the civil war. But questions remained as to whether Iran, a long-standing ally of the Bashar al-Assad regime, would be invited to the negotiations. British Foreign Secretary William Hague said: "I greatly welcome the opposition National Coalition's decision to participate, recognising them as being at the heart and lead of the opposition delegation." The US Secretary of State John Kerry said the Geneva summit offered the best opportunity to bring an end to a conflict that has killed many thousands of people: "We are well aware that the obstacles on the road to a political solution are many, and we will enter the Geneva conference on Syria with our eyes wide open. We will continue to work in concert with the UN and our partners on remaining issues, including which countries will be invited to attend and what the agenda will be."

It was a far cry from the reports coming out of Syria two months earlier in September 2013 when journalist Alison Phillips said: "In the UK's league table of kids we care about, Syria's children are rock bottom." She continued: "Within the pages of coverage on Britain's response to the gassing of civilians in Syria there has been a tidal wave of criticism of our Prime Minister. He has been condemned as a warmonger by some, as America's poodle by others. Others dismissed him simply as a hen-pecked husband meekly responding to SamCam's

[Samantha Cameron's] passionately held views on the situation. But nowhere have I seen the most obvious explanation for his breakneck rush to attack Syria – that he is a parent who has lost a child. He is a man who knows what it is like when the natural order of things breaks down and a parent stands at the grave of their child.

"He is a husband who has had to comfort a wife deprived of her son. He is a father who has had to explain to his children that their sibling has gone. He is, in many ways, just like the parents of the 7,000 children who have been killed so far in the Syrian conflict.

"Last week I travelled to Jordan where I met some of the 130,000 Syrian refugees living in Zaatari camp and saw how they were being supported by Save The Children and other charities. Each had a story of loss and grief. Women just like those I meet on the school run – hairdressers, shop assistants and housewives, but who find themselves living in a war zone. I'm no supporter of David Cameron, never have been. But on this issue I believe he genuinely tried to do the right thing, however ham-fisted that attempt may have been. And I'm sure he was trying to please Barack Obama, too, but it's not George W. Bush in the White House these days. And better that than Ed Miliband's policy of thinking of nothing other than the next election. As a nation we have chosen to turn our collective back on children being killed in Syria. And in doing so we have shown we don't regard dead children in Syria as important as dead children here. And that we don't believe every mother who mourns there does it with the same ferocity as a mother who mourns here.

"Yet can we be so arrogant to think that just because a woman lives in a town we cannot pronounce, in a climate we wouldn't like and follows a religion we don't understand, her love for her babies is less than ours? And that her devastation when they are snuffed out by a shell spewing poisonous gas is somehow less sincere than ours would be? In this country there is national outrage if the system fails to protect just one child – look at the fury around Baby P's death. And rightly so. But if that child happens to live four hours away in Syria we have decided we actively don't want our system helping him. In the UK's league table of kids we care about, Syria's children are rock bottom."

Phillips continued: "Shame on us. I accept we are weary of wars in hot, dusty countries. I accept we cannot know what retaliation a military strike may cause. I accept more people may die as a result of military intervention. But President Assad is a nasty, chinless bully. He has used – or allowed others within his regime to use – poison gases which have caused mass deaths in terrible agony. He has vast stockpiles of this stuff – and as we all know, a bully who isn't challenged will strike again. And again and again. It is only a matter of when Assad will use chemical weapons again – despite them being outlawed by international humanitarian law – because we have sent the signal that we don't really mind.

"We have erased the clear red line about what is acceptable

behaviour and said that we may or may not redraw it at some point in the future, but we're not quite sure when. So in the meantime he is free to stampede across his country and murder his nation's children because we're powerless to stop him. Virtually every family I met in the refugee camp had lost relatives and friends. Syria is now widely regarded as the greatest humanitarian crisis of our generation. Of course, we don't want another prolonged military conflict but short, sharp action would have sent a clear signal to Assad – and ideally destroyed his chemical capability."

The journalist ended her article with: "We have turned our backs on military intervention to help the children. The very least this country can do now is ensure every other possible step is taken to help them through aid and diplomacy – and hope we show more gumption when that next chemical attack rains down."

However, chemical attacks were not the only horror suffered by the children of Syria. On 31st August 2013, The *Sunday Mirror* discovered graphic online footage uploaded by activists that appeared to show youngsters in the capital Damascus suffering from severe malnutrition. Shocking pictures and video showed Syrian children starving to death. The images revealed the horror of families unable to feed their sons and daughters as civil war tore the country apart and the US stood poised to order missile strikes on President Bashar al-Assad's regime. One little boy pictured in a horrific image was believed to be four-year-old Ibrahim Khalil, living in Damascus. Later pictures appeared to show the boy's dead body lying in a mortuary in a besieged suburb of the city. The youngster's plight was revealed by rebel activists on a Facebook page and a YouTube film as the world waited for America's response to the chemical atrocity that left 1,429 people dead, including 426 youngsters. Locals had previously told foreign journalists how they could not afford to eat because food in the war zone was so expensive.

They wanted more handouts from aid agencies, and demanded more money for emergency relief once it was cited that the UK would not be joining any military action. Meanwhile, refugees fleeing the terror flocked to nations bordering Syria, including Lebanon, Iraq and Jordan. Save The Children's response team leader at the Domiz camp in Iraq, Alan Paul, said: "When we have asked refugees who have come over about why they have chosen to come over now, they have mentioned a lack of access to food and water and not feeling confident that they are going to be able to feed their families, and increased fighting." The *Daily Mirror* sparked a worldwide response by publishing pictures of chemical-attack victims on its front page on 22nd August 2013.

Alison Phillips talked to the terrified children at the Zaatari refugee camp near the Syrian border. She wrote: "Yusuf glares defiantly at his mother and says: 'No, I won't go to school.' Schools have been set up at Zaatari refugee camp in Jordan where his family are staying. But Yusuf, seven, won't be going. For him, school means death. And he is understandably terrified. Back home in Syria it was at his school that the 'bad men' came for him: 'I was sitting in class one day with the other kids when they came,' he says, mumbling quietly and staring at the tarpaulin floor of the family's tent. 'They wanted to take me away, to kidnap me. They'd done it to other kids in the past, boys whose dads were fighting in the Syrian free army. They kidnap the boys and say they won't give them back until their fathers hand themselves in.'

"Yusuf's mother Mahal dashed to his school when she heard local thugs had come to the village for her son. As she stormed into the classroom to grab him, fighting broke out and she was shot in the arm. She rolls up her sleeve to show the scar. That day Mahal rescued Yusuf in the confusion. But the family's life became defined by fear.

"Both his parents were vocal critics of the government, making the entire family targets. It wasn't long before the thugs returned for Yusuf at school. 'They grabbed hold of me, then one of them put a grenade around my chest and tucked it inside my shirt,' he says. 'They said to me, "The first time we do this to you we won't detonate it. The second time we do this, we will. Do not come back to school again".'

"Yusuf has the look of a kid a little bit tough, a little bit terrified and hiding all those conflicting emotions with a lot of bravado. When I ask if he was very scared that day he doesn't want to admit it. But slowly he nods. The family struggled on in their home for another couple of months but life only became tougher. 'One day they drove back and forth, back and forth, up and down our street firing at the houses with automatic machine guns,' said

Mahal. 'When they saw it still wasn't making us leave they came back the next day. That's when they poured benzine all round the perimeter of our home and set it on fire. It was all gone.'"

"The family sheltered in a nearby village but rockets exploded around them day and night and finally the family headed for Jordan. 'I didn't want to leave, but we had to' says Yusuf. 'I miss my friends and my father. Back home we'd go to the pool or the amusements or ride round on my bike. It's not nice here. There's too much dust'."

Yusuf did spend time at one of 14 child-friendly spaces created around the camp by Save The Children where children were encouraged to play games and simply be children again. But despite his mother telling him countless times that the school at Zaatari would be safe, he still couldn't fully believe it. "If I go they will find me and put a bomb in my chest" he said. "Or they will capture me and that will put pressure on father to turn himself in."

Yusuf, like thousands of child refugees from Syria, had been forced to grow up too soon by the atrocities he has seen and the trauma of fleeing to another country. Locals called Zaatari the "children's camp". About 60 per cent of the 130,000 people living there were children, and the week before Alison Phillips talked to Yusuf the terrible civil war notched up another sad statistic with its one millionth child refugee. Charities like Save The Children worked tirelessly to make life more tolerable for these children.

Save The Children's Rosie Childs explained: "Many here have endured things no child should see. In our child-friendly spaces our expert teams create a place where they could be anywhere in the world so they can leave the trauma of their experiences behind and start to rebuild their childhood." Yet despite the best efforts of charities the camp still offered a grim childhood, comprised of dusty boredom, sparse rations and searing heat. But 14-year-old Wala'a, for one, was certain it was better than life in Syria. "It is worse there than people can imagine" she said. "Everyone has seen things that they cannot forget. One day I went to my grandfather's house and saw a man shot outside by a sniper. Then at a school near our home a kid wrote something about the regime on the blackboard. The principal came in and said, 'Who wrote this?' but no one would say, so he called the authorities. Soon after, all the fathers of the children were called in and told, 'If you want your children back you have to swap your women for them'. It was for them to be raped."

Such stories can sound almost too extraordinary to be true to western minds but similar accounts were repeated frequently around the camp. Wala'a continues: "My father would go to work in the morning and see garbage bins by the road which bodies of people had been dumped in. Then families of people who had disappeared started getting phone calls saying if they paid a certain amount they could have them back. But when they paid and went to the place as instructed all they found was a bin bag of body parts."

Phillips writes: "Wala'a's gruesome stories seemed incongruous coming from such a strikingly pretty teenager with an infectious giggle bedecked in canary yellow scarf and aqua-painted nails. She is a vivid burst of colour in the bleached-out camp where she arrived seven months ago with her family. Before the fighting started her father had a good job in a factory, she spent weekends hanging out with friends and her evenings studying hard."

Now she was trying to continue with her studies at one of the camp's schools and spent her free time at a centre run by Save The Children for teenage girls where they can take part in sewing and art classes. Back home in Syria, Wala'a once wanted to join the military. That was before she saw the carnage fighting can bring.

"Now I want to be a doctor" she said. "I want to help mend the people hurt by everything that has happened." It would be a major task to even start healing her fellow Syrians' physical and mental wounds. And Wala'a knew it would take a huge international effort. "My mother says, 'Don't worry, everything will be fine, other countries will see what's happening and solve the problem'. I hope so."

While Wala'a's experiences made her passionate and vocal about the situation in Syria – for 12-year-old Farid it has had the opposite effect. He was struck dumb by what he had seen.

"It was one night just over a year ago when the rockets were coming" explained his mother Ibtissam. "We went down to the shelter beneath our house and the noise was incredible. Then one rocket came and hit our home. Farid was terrified.

"When we came up from the shelter we saw our house was destroyed. Farid was shaking violently and could not speak. He didn't speak for months and now he just says the occasional word. Before that night he was funny and playful and talkative. He would have political debates with his aunt when he was only 10. They never agreed and she'd tell him to shut up and he'd tell her, 'No, you shut up'. They were so funny. But now he says barely anything."

Farid's family knew he could talk but that he chose not to. He appeared to have opted out of the violent world he had been forced to endure. For him and the hundreds of thousands of other children who had fled Syria, the adult world of bombs and guns was somewhere they simply did not want to be.

After three years of conflict the toll on Syrian children and their families had been enormous. Alison Phillips wrote: "We utterly condemn the use of chemical weapons as a crime, but urge that whatever course of action is decided, that children be prioritised, protected and kept safe from harm."

Save The Children had helped more than 600,000 children and families in Syria and the region, but the needs continued to be huge. Phillips said: "At this critical moment, the international community must not avert its gaze from the humanitarian catastrophe. We urgently need unimpeded access to all parts of Syria and much greater funding by the international community, if we are to respond to the worst refugee crisis for a generation."

In June 2012 the *Daily Mirror*'s political editor, Jason Beattie, wrote: "Tiny corpses lie side by side after another atrocity blamed on the Syrian government's death squads." World leaders heaped more pressure at the time on President al-Assad after opposition groups said that 100 people – including 20 women and children – had been murdered in their homes. "Videos posted online showed some of the bodies that were recovered from the rubble of the devastated village of al-Qubair." One dead boy appeared to have been shot in the face. Human rights campaigners said that pro-Assad militia – known as the Shabiha – ran amok after the area had been shelled by regular forces for five hours. Horrified villager Leith al-Hamwy said the militiamen "killed and hacked everyone they could find". Beattie wrote: "He said his family – his mum and six siblings, the youngest being 10-year-old twins – were burned to death when the thugs torched their home. Leith survived by hiding in an olive grove 800 yards from the farms as the troops went berserk." He said: "When I came out of hiding and went in the houses I saw bodies everywhere. Entire families were shot dead or killed with sharp sticks and knives. The atrocity in Hama province came two weeks after 108 innocent people were butchered by the Shabiha in Houla. Syrian forces shot at UN monitors trying to reach al-Qubair. The UN Secretary General, Ban Ki-moon, told the UN General Assembly in New York that the massacre was an act of "unspeakable barbarity", adding that Assad's government had "lost all legitimacy". The opposition

Syrian National Council reported the number of dead, while an activist in Hama said: "The troops executed nearly every person in the village. Very few could flee. Most were slaughtered with knives in a horrible way." The US Secretary of State Hilary Clinton said she was disgusted by the "regime-sponsored violence" and repeated that Assad should go. Meanwhile, President al-Assad's "monster" vanished with the remains of the slaughtered victims, roaming Syria committing atrocity after atrocity. The death squads had swooped on villages and massacred women and children by slitting their throats or shooting them at point-blank range. They then disappeared with the hacked remains in an effort to cover up their brutality. However experts said there was no mistaking the sickening work. Dressed in their unofficial uniform of combat trousers and black T-shirts, the muscle-bound thugs were undoubtedly the "butchers of Assad's regime". Armed with AK47s and machetes, they travelled behind the military, and after the army stopped shelling towns "Ghosts" swarmed in to kill any survivors. They were paid around £130 a day – a fortune in Syria – with funds coming from businessmen who supported the President's regime.

Established in the 1970s, they were a Mafia-style gang in the coastal port of Latakia, the centre of the Assad family power base. "They used to smuggle weapons and drugs, but now they are butchers" said Michael Weiss, a Syria expert at the UK-based Henry Jackson Society. In return for letting them operate above the law, the Shabiha act as Assad's enforcers. The "Ghosts" were fanatical followers of the Muslim Alawite sect, which ruled the country and had been brainwashed into thinking the Sunni majority were the enemy. In 2013, the Shabiha were told that they were fighting for their lives because they would face revenge if the regime was ever overthrown. The men are frightening – tall, with huge muscles, bearded and tanked up on steroids, which have pumped up their bodies. After the attack in al-Qubair, the Syrian army boasted of "cleansing" the town by capturing it from rebel forces. The regime said it had restored "peace and security", killing a "large number" of "terrorists" fighting against Assad's troops.